MW01005608

If life has been suffocating and your day-t[...] genrader provides a God-breathed breath [...] *Four Habits for Faithful Living.* In a comp[...] the asphyxiating smog of an overwhelmin[...] anxious me with Gospel restoration and Spirit-given tools for refreshment. The journey is fun, interesting, and inspiring. If your soul needs some oxygen, open the windows of your life, breathe in her words, and receive the gifts Jesus shares generously through His life-giving Spirit.

—Rev. Michael W. Newman, author of *Getting Through Grief* and *Hope When Your Heart Breaks*; president, Texas District, LCMS

If asked to describe *Inspired by the Holy Spirit* in three words, I'd choose *refreshing*, *relatable*, and *relevant*. Like a breath of fresh air, this book will refresh and inspire you, drawing you closer to God's love and grace. As Christina shares her life openly, honestly, and vulnerably, you will find yourself relating to her struggles, as well as enjoying the fun, creative challenges for each day's reading. The truths shared are relevant for all times, whether a past experience that has been long since forgotten or fresh from the day before. If you are looking for inspiration and a renewed soul, this is the book for you!

—Kathy Cowan, director of women's ministry, Memorial Lutheran Church, Katy, Texas

Are you yearning for spiritual transformation? Through *Inspired by the Holy Spirit*, author Christina Hergenrader helps you connect with the Counselor, who leads us to a deeper relationship with God. Along the way, you'll learn how reading God's Word can be a well of hydration for the soul and not just a source of information. How prayer holds the key to finding the missing "peace" in your life. How the habit of praise attunes you to the wonder of God's promises and relentless love. How you can reflect God's glory and grace by using the gifts and talents He has given you. Start reading this book and you'll immediately feel like you've just met a new sister in Christ who willingly shares her vulnerabilities just so she can encourage you to hang on to God for dear, sweet life.

—Sharla Fritz, author of *God's Relentless Love*

Inspired by the Holy Spirit hit me like a refreshing jump into a pool on a hot day. More than once, I felt that Christina must have been peering into the windows of my own home and soul, as I was convicted and comforted by her description of the journey on which she invites her readers to join her. The beauty is that it's simply an invitation to remember who we are as the beloved children of God by prioritizing those places where He has promised His Spirit will be present and active in our lives. I think this journey will be incredibly valuable to the students and staff where I teach, to their parents, to my own wife and daughters, and to children of God from all walks of life.

—Rev. Aaron Richert, campus pastor, Lutheran South Academy, Houston, Texas

Reading *Inspired by the Holy Spirit* helped the Holy Spirit speak straight to my heart. There were many days I felt the author was speaking directly to my experiences and struggles. It illuminates the everyday barriers that keep us from recognizing the Holy Spirit's transforming work in our lives and gives practical steps for seeking inspiration from Scripture, in worship, in prayer, and through service. If you've been looking for a way to strengthen your daily spiritual life, I highly recommend this study.

—Laura Hemminger, mom, former director of Y4Life at Lutherans For Life

Christina Hergenrader's *Inspired by the Holy Spirit* presents an honest and beautiful look at living a Spirit-filled life. Her human confessions ("In my most insecure moments, I am a black-belt coveter") make me smile and identify. But at the same time, her awareness of God's presence stuns in a way you can almost feel: "These moments hum with the knowledge that something holy is happening." Practical applications give the reader an increased awareness of how the Holy Spirit works in and through us. Reading this book will leave you *inspired*!

—Mary Fuller, artist, author, Bible teacher

Inspired by the Holy Spirit: Four Habits for Faithful Living is twenty-eight days of short, easy-to-read, thought-provoking messages, things to do, challenges, and prayers. Author Christina Hergenrader uses real-life examples and relevant Bible verses. She tells how to use this study for individuals, small groups, and large groups, focusing on (1) God's Word, (2) prayer, (3) praise, and (4) reflection. I really liked her statement, "Describing spiritual transformation can sometimes feel like doing card tricks on the radio." So true—and yet so worth it! Read this book to gain insight on how to lead your best spirit-filled life.

—Judy Keetle, retired educator

INSPIRED
by the HOLY SPIRIT

Four Habits for Faithful Living

Christina Hergenrader

CONCORDIA PUBLISHING HOUSE • SAINT LOUIS

Dedication

Dad, thank you for all your hours of research, for our constant theological conversations, for your humbleness, and for your curiosity. If all that was so this book could be born, then it was worth it.

Mom, thank you for your example of hospitality, of connecting, of praying, of quiet sacrifice, of intuition, and for being funny. You are a model of spiritual living, and we are so blessed to have you here.

Published by Concordia Publishing House
3558 S. Jefferson Ave., St. Louis, MO 63118-3968
1-800-325-3040 • cph.org

Copyright © 2021 Christina Hergenrader

Unless otherwise indicated, Scripture quotations from the ESV® Bible (The Holy Bible, English Standard Version®), copyright © 2001 by Crossway, a publishing ministry of Good News Publishers. Used by permission. All rights reserved.

Hymns marked *LSB* are from *Lutheran Service Book*, copyright © 2006 Concordia Publishing House. All rights reserved.

Cover images: © 2021 shutterstock.com

Manufactured in the United States of America

1   2   3   4   5   6   7   8   9   10   30   29   28   27   26   25   24   23   22   21

Contents

How to Use This Book

Welcome, new friend. We'll be spending the next four weeks together, learning more each day about how to live our best Spirit-filled life. Get ready for something different. This experience with God's Word and the love of Jesus will change the way you see yourself and the way you see the Holy Spirit.

A word of caution, though—describing spiritual transformation can sometimes feel like doing card tricks on the radio. Words don't describe the miracle. So we'll be doing daily challenges, telling one another the stories of what we discover, and noticing all the ways the Holy Spirit inspires change in ordinary days.

Get ready for an *experience*.

To get the most from this guide, decide the best way to use it: as an individual study, as a small accountability-group study, or as a large-group experience.

Whichever you choose, give it your all. Trust that God is working through His Word to show you who Jesus is and how the Holy Spirit, who was given to you in your Baptism, gives you the power to live out your faith.

The more you put into this study, the more you'll get out of it. And isn't that why you're here? To experience a deeper change, to find what life is about, and to live your best Spirit-filled life.

Individual Study

Welcome to your best spiritual life. *Inspired* is a four-week study that you read every day. My hope is that this study will help you live more fully in God's love and the power of the Holy Spirit. Each day includes stories, challenges, questions, and prayer to help you grow in your faith and passion for the beautiful life God has given you.

1. Plan your week around how you are going to read every day's devotion and complete the activities. Set aside about thirty minutes for your daily study. Write answers to the reflection questions. Keep a journal of your thoughts, prayers, and questions. Like most things, you will get out of this what you put into it. Carve out the time and space to devote yourself to this study.

2. Keep your Bible handy for your daily devotion time. You'll also want to have a pen, journal, and your copy of this book nearby.

3. Remember that when you live a more inspired life, you are soaking up the work of the Holy Spirit. God promises that when you pray to Him in faith, He always answers that prayer (Matthew 21:22). But change can be so uncomfortable—seriously, it can make you want to stop and do something way easier. Please keep showing up and doing this study. Don't give up the habit of reading and answering the

questions. Check in with someone who will keep you accountable.

4. Plan your time:

- Spend twenty minutes (of your thirty-minute time) with the daily reading. Look up the Bible verses. Mark up the story in the devotion with your reactions and insights and questions. Answer the questions. Make a plan for doing the daily challenge. Finally, pray and note any prayer requests you have (for example, about your own day, about how God is working in your life, and about what people in your life need).

- Use about eight minutes to journal about what you see unfolding in your life. What do you hope God will change? How are your actions not in line with His Word? What new habits and faith growth do you hope will happen? The more specific you are here, the more effective it will be. Be brave, my dear! Tell it like it is and be honest and vulnerable about what you want and what you need from your heavenly Father.

- Take two minutes to look ahead to the next day. Read the challenge and note how you can set yourself up for success.

Small Accountability-Group Bible Study

1. If you use this guide as a small-group study, gather your friends, family, neighbors, and sisters in Christ and figure out a time and place that works for all of you. One person in the group should lead the

meeting and keep things on track and on time. The leader can be someone different each week.

Consider kicking off your study with the large-group event described on page 10. A meal or experience can set the tone for the next month together. This will be an exciting journey together, so begin it with an intentional gathering of your group. You'll be sharing stories, time, prayers, and encouragement. Celebrate what's about to begin.

2. Before you meet each week, read the introduction and the six daily devotions for the week ahead. You will do this prep work in your own personal Bible study time. Be sure to answer all the questions. Try the challenges. Write down your thoughts and experiences. Be ready to share all of this with your group during your weekly meeting.

    Of course, your first meeting will be slightly different than the others. When you come together for the first week, you'll read the introduction to the book (page 19) together. Also, at your first meeting, look ahead over the format of this study. Ask each woman to share about her schedule and when she plans to work through her daily homework.

3. For your time together every week, bring your copy of *Inspired by the Holy Spirit: Four Habits for Faithful Living*, your Bible, your notes, and a pen.

4. During your meetings, share your experiences with each of the daily challenges. Be ready to tell your accountability group about how these spiritual rhythms are shaping your faith.

5. Keep one another accountable. As you all share this experience together, encourage one another to keep up with the reading and questions. Commit to calling or texting your group. Check in with those who are struggling. Pray for one another.

6. Plan your time with your small group accordingly:

- About 70 percent of your time should be spent talking about the previous week's reading. Share with the group how the week went for you. Which daily readings and activities did you find to be helpful? Which challenges were hard for you? What did you learn?

  (Note that part of this 70 percent is answering all the questions from the previous week. Each day has three questions, and there are seven days. The leader should randomly ask for people to share their reactions, fears, challenges, and blessings that came through these questions.)

- About 20 percent of the time should be talking about the introduction to this week's focus of inspired living. Discuss the habit and where you currently find yourself with this particular part of inspired living. Answer the questions in the introduction.

- About 10 percent of the time should be spent looking ahead to the next week and how it may be different for each person. Look at the daily challenges to see what they involve. Check with one another about what highlights and hardships are coming in the week ahead. Plan for daily time in the study and in God's Word.

Large-Group Study for Retreats and Events, as Well as a Kickoff

Use this guide to present *Inspired by the Holy Spirit: Four Habits for Faithful Living* as part of any retreat, women's event, or prayer breakfast. You can also teach *Inspired* for a large group as a one-day online event. You can tailor this to use as a Zoom Bible study or a Facebook Live retreat.

Inspired works very well for a large-group study. If you are leading this as a women's event, weekend retreat topic, Sunday morning class, or one-day Bible study, consider the following program to inspire the women in your church or community.

> (Please note—you can also use this one-day retreat as a kickoff for your accountability group. If your church or women's group plans to study this book for the next month, you can begin the study with the following overview. Pair the presentation with a meal, invite a crowd, and build excitement about the study.)

1. As you plan your large-group event, think about ways you can connect the theme of inspired living to the setting, food, decorations, and tone of the event. Inspired living means celebrating the love of Jesus and the power of the Spirit in your life. Use music, art, worship, Bible verses, and thought-provoking questions to set the tone for the event.

2. The presentation portion of your large-group event will take about sixty minutes. As a guide, please use

the following estimates to create the best experience for the women who attend this large-group event:

- Spend twenty to twenty-five minutes on presenting the concept of inspired living. Read parts of the introduction that explain how the power of the Holy Spirit can change every part of our lives. Talk about how God works through these four habits to make us more aware of our identity as God's daughters and of the Spirit's power in each of our lives.

- For the next twenty-five minutes, break down each of the four habits:

   —reading God's Word and applying it to your life;
   —praying aloud, with a group, in solitude, or with a prayer journal;
   —reflecting and listening to God through journaling, through conversation with another believer, through service, and through ways the Spirit changes our actions; and
   —worshiping God in a personal, contemplative way or in a collective group way.

- For ten minutes, challenge women to consider the parts of their lives they would like to improve. You can use these questions to prompt small or large group discussion:

   —Is your worry stealing your joy?
   —Is it hard for you to make decisions?
   —Do you feel powerless or stuck?
   —What about your life do you want God to transform?
   —What creative challenges have you done lately?

—Are you hoping to find new spiritual habits to guide
your life?

—Have you fallen out of the habit of prayer, worship,
and Bible study?

- For the final five minutes, describe the next steps women
  can take to live more inspired lives. Encourage them to
  join an *Inspired* study, to use the book for their personal
  Bible study time, to connect with an accountability part-
  ner who will help them see the power of the Holy Spirit
  in their lives, and to welcome the transformation of God's
  power to help each of them better understand His love for
  them.

- Obviously, you will want to include God's Word, prayer,
  and collective and contemplative worship in your event.
  After all, this retreat is about living a more inspired life.
  That means celebrating the Holy Spirit's work in your life
  right now. Structure your time together to include all of
  these.

- Suggested Bible verses include the following:

If you love Me, you will keep My commandments.
And I will ask the Father, and He will give you
another Helper, to be with you forever, even the
Spirit of truth, whom the world cannot receive,
because it neither sees Him nor knows Him. You
know Him, for He dwells with you and will be in
you. I will not leave you as orphans; I will come
to you. (John 14:15–18)

These things I have spoken to you while I am still
with you. But the Helper, the Holy Spirit, whom

the Father will send in My name, He will teach you all things and bring to your remembrance all that I have said to you. (John 14:25–26)

But when the Helper comes, whom I will send to you from the Father, the Spirit of truth, who proceeds from the Father, He will bear witness about Me. (John 15:26)

Nevertheless, I tell you the truth: it is to your advantage that I go away, for if I do not go away, the Helper will not come to you. But if I go, I will send Him to you. . . . I still have many things to say to you, but you cannot bear them now. When the Spirit of truth comes, He will guide you into all the truth, for He will not speak on His own authority, but whatever He hears He will speak, and He will declare to you the things that are to come. He will glorify Me, for He will take what is Mine and declare it to you. (John 16:7, 12–14)

The Helper, the Holy Spirit, reminds each of us of God's love. This reminder is such a comfort. When life is frantic, it's easy to lose focus on what has real value. In the moments when we desperately need help, the Holy Spirit reminds us not to return evil for evil, reminds us how to pray, and reminds us how to show God's love to the world. He sustains us in the faith and brings the deep peace that comes from forgiveness.

For the Holy Spirit will teach you in that very hour what you ought to say. (Luke 12:12)

Likewise the Spirit helps us in our weakness. For we do not know what to pray for as we ought, but the Spirit Himself intercedes for us with groanings too deep for words. And He who searches hearts knows what is the mind of the Spirit, because the Spirit intercedes for the saints according to the will of God. (Romans 8:26–27)

But the fruit of the Spirit is love, joy, peace, patience, kindness, goodness, faithfulness, gentleness, self-control; against such things there is no law. (Galatians 5:22–23)

To set the mind on the Spirit is life and peace. (Romans 8:6)

May the God of hope fill you with all joy and peace in believing, so that by the power of the Holy Spirit you may abound in hope. (Romans 15:13)

Good News! I Can Join You!

Although any speaker can invigorate your group about living a more inspired life, I do travel to speak and love it very much. If your group would prefer a Zoom event or webinar for your large group gathering, I am also happy to do that. Please contact me on Facebook, Instagram, or by email at christina@christinasbooks.com.

First, a Word about These Strange, Strange Times

The birth of this book—of this new way of living—coincided eerily and perfectly with the birth of COVID-19 in our world. Please know that the words on these pages were forged during the most perplexing time in recent history.

That timing is significant, I believe. One lesson I've learned about living more spiritually is that the timing is *always* significant. Indeed, peculiar timing is one of the ways that the Holy Spirit seems to work in our lives.

Prior to this pandemic, something had been missing for all of us for quite some time. We (the Church, current culture, humans, all of it) were too harried. Too busy, yes. But more than that. We were spiritually bankrupt. We kept visiting the empty wells in an effort to be made whole.

It felt as if so many of us had propped up our ladders against the wrong buildings. While we seemed to be climbing higher, it was to reach the wrong places. So many of us were investing more and more in something that would numb the deep ache we felt. We tried getting busier, wealthier, more distracted, angrier, more successful. But these ladders did not give us more guidance or love or meaning. They had led us to a great fall.

I know you understand what I'm describing because we were all feeling it. Dry bones everywhere. We were thirsty for spiritual nourishment.

At the end of February 2020, I was in southern California to speak at several churches. It was a different scene then than it would be in the next month. No one had heard the phrase *social distancing*, and in all the places I traveled, zero people wore masks or had even heard of this new coronavirus.

On my flight back to Texas, I submitted to my editor a rough outline of a book I wanted to write about living more soulfully. My proposal was vague because I couldn't quite form my thoughts about what this new way of living needed to be.

But here's the image that kept coming to me: Christians are gorging themselves on so much information, too much hustle, loads of cynicism, and lots of pride. We keep shoveling in more, more, more. Meanwhile, all we really need is one small, simple meal of real nourishment.

What did that meal look like, though? No one needed more advice or research or self-help. What we all needed was a picture, a model, an example of something different. We needed the source itself. We needed the Holy Spirit and a life centered around Jesus Christ.

I prayed to live this out exactly. "Let me live my life differently, Lord. Transform me so I can be a model of what sacred rhythms look like in an actual life." I asked God over and over to crack my hard exoskeleton of humanness and infuse me with His Holy Spirit so I could figure out how to live out this experience and then write this book.

Then I got sick, and my family did too. We spent the next week sleeping and coughing and wondering why we felt so bad. Of course, the answer was all over the news. Slowly—and then all at once—COVID-19 shut down our family's lives. And then COVID shut down *everything*.

By this time, we were deep into March—scared and perplexed over how this virus was damaging the lives and health of so many people. You were there; I don't need to rehash the details except to say that in the span of one week, our calendar went from looking like a game of Tetris to being totally and completely empty.

It was unbelievable.

I realize now that we were only a couple of steps into what would be a marathon.

Scientists scrambled to understand the virus. The media haunted us all with predictions and conclusions—many of which never came true. Social media screamed with fear and anger and deep, deep grief. The word *unprecedented* suddenly became the most commonly used word in the world.

It was too much. Our minds couldn't keep up with the changes in the news every day. Our relationships buckled under the pressure of not seeing one another. Everywhere, everyone was arguing. It was like all the anxiety knobs were turned all the way up, and we could not escape the fear.

I still had a book to write, and that meant I needed to find answers to what was making all of us so sick—and I don't mean the virus that made masks the year's top fashion accessory.

I mean why were our souls so sick?

Now, more than ever, I wanted to understand a different way to live.

Amid all our systems breaking, our plans constantly pivoting, and no hope for the old reality to return, I saw what I needed to find my answers. I took on this quarantined life with the desperation I had been carrying around everywhere.

With COVID came my invitation for a life in the Spirit. And I grabbed it.

This book then wrote itself as I shed more and more of what had been cluttering my life. Much, much less social media, less spending money to make me feel in control, fewer fake answers. I became more vulnerable in prayer, and I got lots and lots of rest.

This is what I learned: this one holy and precious life from your heavenly Father is your invitation to freedom and meaning and peace. The Holy Spirit gives you the life of Jesus Christ. You take on His forgiveness, righteousness, peace, and victory through the Word and Sacraments, Baptism and the Lord's Supper.

This is what you want.

This is what you need.

This guide is what it looks like to live it.

May you live the life you have been given. May you turn to prayer constantly. May you keep burrowing deeper into His Word to find real strength. May your very life and all you create give glory to the one true Savior. May you notice the ways the Spirit nudges you toward the gifts of real goodness, divine patience, and deep love.

Introduction: Parched, Hungry, and Why You're Here

Hi, my dear friend.

There's a reason you've picked up this book—and I can guess what it might be.

You're feeling worn out. You're looking for something more. Money doesn't relieve the deep aching. Every relationship is complicated. Your day is filled with so much hustle and not nearly enough connection or curiosity or depth. The old systems and routines aren't working anymore. You don't feel very alive. At the end of all this striving and working and pushing, there is always more work.

You want a deeper, more creative, joy-filled, invigorating life. You want the real meat of what's true. You're feeling hungry for deeper connection with someone who's not on a screen. You want something sacred.

I wanted all of that too. And the pages of this book—this month-long experience—are all those things. This guide will lead you in immersing yourself in inspiration, divine joy, and real depth.

Here is the only real inspiration—and it turns out to be everything. You are the beloved child of God. In your identity in Christ are the answers to who you are and who you have always been. In this place, we will dig in and discover the riches of who He is.

For the next four weeks, you will learn new habits. You'll rebuild your life from the deepest part of you—your soul. You'll detox from the bad habits you've fallen into. Throughout this month, we'll spend a week talking about the habit of reading God's Word, then a week on prayer, then worship, and finally reflection.

Every day, you'll read a devotion that describes a part of what's happening in your spiritual journey. You'll dig deeper with discussion and journaling questions. You'll also have a daily challenge to develop this new habit. And you'll end your devotion time in prayer.

Restructure your life from hustle to rest, from rules to creativity, from information to inspiration. Rethink all those to-do lists, and aim for deep spiritual nourishment.

That parched feeling is your soul craving more from God's Word, more worship, more time in prayer. Your heart and mind will rejoice when reflecting on Christ's redemptive, renewing, regenerating work in your life that comes to you in that Word and in worship as you hear the Gospel preached and as you receive the Lord's Supper.

Join me on this adventure. God will inspire you, and that will change everything.

Onward, into our month together.

Christina Hergenrader
ChristinaHergenrader.com

WORD

Inspired in the Word: Introduction

Now we have received not the spirit of the world, but the Spirit who is from God, that we might understand the things freely given us by God. And we impart this in words not taught by human wisdom but taught by the Spirit, interpreting spiritual truths to those who are spiritual. The natural person does not accept the things of the Spirit of God, for they are folly to him, and he is not able to understand them because they are spiritually discerned. . . . "For who has understood the mind of the Lord so as to instruct Him?" But we have the mind of Christ. (1 Corinthians 2:12–14, 16)

My brain has been trying to save me for as long as I can remember. It's very good at reading, learning, memorizing, and constantly clicking life into categories—avoid this; do more of that; remember this, it will be helpful later. My mind is constantly processing information. It believes it's guarding me from danger.

Maybe you're the same way. Maybe your brain never stops analyzing and warning and, well, freaking out. Maybe you are also constantly scanning and scrolling and looking for more information. And there's never been a better time to love input, right?

Before you eat breakfast, you've already ingested the top headlines from around the world, chewed on the morning's political debate, and tasted the bitter feelings served up on social media through a constant scroll of memes and posts.

And that's not even what's happening in your own home. More anxiety is waiting there. Like mine, your brain has worked for decades to keep you safe. God created our minds for many purposes, one of which is to police our environment and to spot and react to any kind of danger. Your brain is so good at its job.

This is also where the problem comes in, though. Or, rather, this is where the angst comes in. Because your mind is also a bad neighborhood of pain and projection and hurtful memories. Does this scenario sound familiar to you?

In the morning, you walk through your kitchen and see the blob of jelly on the counter from breakfast—the counter you asked your husband to wipe off before you left for work. You see the leftover muffins and feel guilty that you ate three of them. After all, you promised yourself that this was the week you would have egg-white omelets for breakfast. (By the way, that declaration sounds just like your mother, who is always promising herself to eat healthier. That's how her weight has crept up. You're probably just like her, destined for insulin shots and blood pressure medicine.)

You're not even to your computer yet, and your mind has already created scenarios of anxiety and warnings of hopelessness. And this comes just from the stuff lying around in your kitchen.

You see the problem with this. None of it is reality. These are the weird, damaged, highly fearful perspectives of our sin-infected brains. Our busy minds are so constantly filled with information that they never stop clicking away with ways life isn't working, and how life could be better, and one million other facts and opinions and dangers.

Recently, I felt worn out by this anxiety my mind was creating. After one weird, long day when my brain felt as if it were in a toxic spiral of so much worry, I searched the internet for ways to feel calmer. (Ha, of course; why not reach out for another strategy, when I'm already drowning in plans and schemes?) I came across Paul's words in 2 Corinthians 2.

In his Second Letter to the Corinthians, Paul writes about how Christians, who are filled with the Holy Spirit, have the mind of Christ. This mind is so different from an anxious mind. My mind is filled with worry because of my sin. But because of God's love, the Spirit makes me new. This means that I have real security, I know real love, and I understand real forgiveness. This means I have the peace-filled mind of Christ. That means that I'm not only my thoughts and fears—I'm something so much more.

Ah. When I read Paul's words, they pierced me. I had been gorging on information when what I was really hungry for was spiritual nourishment. Something changed here. Reading these words was like putting on a new pair of glasses.

My life was bloated with information, and I could now see the weakness of it all. I finally understood that I am not my thoughts. These new glasses let me see that I have been made new in Christ. More information and more thinking won't help me. It's not what I need.

You too. Jesus Christ has made you new through the Spirit. The new you doesn't hold on to shame or remember sin or feel tortured with what it isn't accomplishing. Instead, it is marinating in the peace that surpasses understanding (Philippians 4:7).

This helped me see how I read my Bible all wrong. And so I began to understand God's Word with eyes not just for more information to analyze and apply and make me feel guilty. The Word of God is most importantly Gospel—information to soothe and comfort my guilty, fearful mind with the balm of forgiveness and grace that Jesus provides. God's holy and precious Word is food for the soul, which is starving for real sustenance.

When I read Jesus' words now, my heart, mind, and soul soak up this message. Over and over, Jesus is talking to His disciples, to the crowds, and to us about our *spiritual* needs. Jesus keeps saying what it means to follow Him.

For so long, my brain read the Beatitudes through a lens of guilt. My mind read how I cannot even get close to being meek because I have so many problems being humble, and how I'm never a peacemaker because I really secretly love to watch drama unfold.

Again with the analyzing and guilt. These are not verses to make me feel anxious because Jesus clearly wasn't talking about what I needed to do for God to love me—He was talking about what I do now that He has made me a new creation. We belong to God. Jesus' words are for those who have been transformed by the Spirit.

In John 15:26, Jesus tells the disciples that when the Spirit of truth comes, He will shed light on everything He said and did. We have that Spirit of truth, and that's how we read the Bible now. Reading the Bible is vital to how you live in this world. The words Paul used to describe Scripture are "breathed out by God" (2 Timothy 3:16). The writers of Scripture "spoke from God as they were carried along by the Holy Spirit" (2 Peter 1:21). The promise of Jesus to send the Spirit is a promise of love that you need every day. This promise is not more information—it is love.

Let's dive into the Word of God together. Let's look at these verses and receive the message of love that is deeper than understanding and better than the terrible ranting of your bully brain. Let's read these verses through the lens of our faith, through the eyes of completely loved, forgiven, and redeemed creatures.

This daily habit of reading God's Word is nutrition for your soul. Your brain will try to hijack every morning, every moment of your life. Infuse it with this reminder that you are a beloved child of God that He is restoring and renewing by that nutrition.

For Today

1. When do you find yourself trapped in the spiral of information? What false hope does this give you? How is the Word of God different?

2. Read Deuteronomy 11:18–21 and talk (or write) about this description of total immersion in the Word of God. What would life be like if you counted on the Word of God as much as you count on other information?

3. As you begin this study, pray for the Holy Spirit to illuminate your life with God's Word. Ask your heavenly Father for wisdom and inspiration as you make this habit part of your daily routine.

This Week

If you're feeling addicted to information, your soul is malnourished. This week, you'll have the chance to soak up the Good News of God's love for you. Rest in His promises, and invite the Spirit to transform you in heart, mind, and soul.

Pray

Come, Holy Spirit; give me new breath and life. Fill me with Your inspiration and change my life. Help me, Lord, to come to You for encouragement and love. In Jesus' name, I pray. Amen.

NEVER LOSE THIS

Even the Spirit of truth, whom the world cannot receive, because it neither sees Him nor knows Him. You know Him, for He dwells with you and will be in you. (John 14:17)

We have three teenagers at home right now. Catie, our oldest, turned sixteen this summer. Sam and Elisabeth are our thirteen-year-old twins. When our ten-year-old, Nate, is thirteen, we will have four teenagers living in the house. We will need our names on all your best prayer chains.

I'm totally kidding because actually, teenagers are really fun. Yes, they use a lot of our WiFi bandwith, and they seem to drip clothes and bags and cords and food all over the house. But they are also so funny and great at dancing in the kitchen and are absolutely exploding with thoughts and insights and self-discovery and good (or sometimes not so good) ideas.

Just like the toddler years, adolescence brings mistakes and failures and finding the right footing. Sometimes it looks easy; other times, it's about as graceful as the middle-school dances our twins are suddenly interested in.

It's during these intense times of self-discovery that we mamas and aunts and grandmas are on our knees, praying for our family. We are praying they will stay close to God forever.

But there's more to it.

I don't want my kids to lose their awe about our God, who made us so wonderfully. I pray every day that as they become concrete thinkers, with their own opinions, they don't abandon the wonder of our Creator working in divine ways through the most ordinary materials. Because now is the time—as they form a deeper understanding of who God is—that they might decide they can only believe in what has proof and form and deliberate function.

Maybe you know what I'm talking about because this has happened to you. There was a time when you weren't shy to pray spontaneously because you totally trusted that God was right there, His divinity humming like a motor in your soul. Or you saw everything in your life as a gift from God and never questioned that He put it here to delight or help you. Most importantly, perhaps, you could feel the dramatic peace that God gave you. Terrified in bed at night, you would pray and then immediately know—without a doubt—that the deep calm you felt was straight from God.

But then, you got older and learned about the world's history and that rainbows are a promise from God but also a result of sunlight reflecting the moisture in the atmosphere. Maybe you discovered that some people say they're Christian because it serves them, but in reality, they are evil and hurtful.

As you learned more—about how broken the world is or how science seems to have an explanation for so much of what looks like miracles—you might have abandoned all of the spiritual wonder in favor of a safer, more logical, structured faith.

Or, perhaps, you left behind your faith in a God who loves you and provides for all your needs, and you planted yourself firmly in the "I can take care of myself" camp.

Don't do that. Don't throw away the childlike awe you once had. Trust that your faith wasn't silliness or immaturity or stupidity, but real. The truth is that God is caring for His entire creation, and He gave us His Son out of His deep love for us. Trust that those moments of peace after reading God's Word, hearing the Absolution after confessing your sins, or receiving Christ's body and blood in Holy Communion are *real*.

Trust that what God tells us about the Holy Spirit is true and marvelous and thrilling. In John 14:16–17, Jesus says that the Father is sending "the Spirit of truth" to help us and live in us.

This Holy Spirit created faith in you and made His home in you through Baptism. This Spirit inspired His Word and uses those Scriptures to strengthen that faith. The Holy Spirit nourishes us through the body and blood of Jesus Christ in Holy Communion. "The Spirit Himself intercedes for us with groanings too deep for words" (Romans 8:26).

This constancy of the Spirit is part of every single moment of every single day. Quit telling yourself that you're imagining it, and instead, take God at His Word when He says, "Faith is . . . the conviction of things not seen" (Hebrews 11:1). Your childlike faith is a gift to understand this very good news. The Holy Spirit that came to you in Baptism is a new pair of glasses to see the world through eyes of faith.

Never lose this. Never doubt that Jesus' love, God's wisdom, and the Holy Spirit's power are part of who you are now. As you grow and discover and mature and learn more about this world, never lose the eyes of faith that help you see that all of it—your Baptism, your experiences, your Savior's death and resurrection, and your whole self—are a gift from your heavenly Father.

For Today

1. Tell your faith story. When have you found yourself relying more on yourself than on God? When have you focused more on earthly things than on heavenly things? Explain.

2. Read John 14:26; John 16:7–8, 13; Acts 1:8; Ephesians 1:13, 17–20; Romans 8:10–11, 26–27. What does the Holy Spirit do in your life? Make a list from these verses.

3. This week, write in your prayer journal about the areas of your daily life in which you struggle to believe. Ask God to strengthen you with the Holy Spirit to trust Him and to love others.

Challenge!

For today, notice where God is working in your life through the eyes of faith. When you see His work, send yourself a text. Note what happened every time you put the fruit of the Spirit into action (love, joy, peace, patience, kindness, goodness, faithfulness, gentleness, and self-control; see Galatians 5:22–23).

Pray

Lord of everything, help me to see Your power in my life. Inspire me to see Your goodness and promises throughout every part of my day. Give me Your Spirit to know You better, Father. In Your Son's name, I pray. Amen.

DAY 4

SHAME GOGGLES

Create in me a clean heart, O God, and renew a right spirit within me. Cast me not away from Your presence, and take not Your Holy Spirit from me. Restore to me the joy of Your salvation, and uphold me with a willing spirit. (Psalm 51:10-12)

Like everyone else in the world, during the Great Pause of 2020, we adopted a puppy. Why not? Thanks to COVID, we were home all the time. We were already wearing out our beloved old greyhound, Jack, with about sixteen walks a day. If not spreading COVID meant locking ourselves away from everyone else, then we would lock ourselves up with an energetic young Greyhound and all of his shenanigans. Super idea, right?

Eh, kind of. Red, our new one-year-old Greyhound rescue, had the energy of a toddler on espresso. He literally ran the length of our house most of the day. When he had tired out the four kids, he would hunt in our closets for tennis shoes, leather belts, and baseball caps to chew on.

Also, Red did not quite get the hang of the whole potty-outside rule. He tried; he really did. But he had been raised with the rest of his litter of racing Greyhounds on a farm that encouraged dogs to make themselves at home and relieve themselves wherever was most convenient.

Anyone who has ever tried to teach a dog that the carpet is not grass knows that old habits die hard. So we turned to what the best trainers on the internet could teach us. Kennel him when we leave. Restrict access to his favorite places to urinate. Never stop watching him. Install a doggy door in the off-chance he might want to go out when one of us wasn't waiting to open the door.

When none of that worked, we invested in a multipack of cleaning cloths and super-strong chemicals to neutralize the smell of urine, all in hopes that Red would stop sneaking into my office and marking it as his own.

The carpet cleaners worked pretty well, and so did the other tricks. However, nothing helped Red learn where to potty as well as shame did. Red came to recognize the big red-and-white sanitizing bottle as a symbol of his failure. And our puppy really hated to disappoint us.

Whenever I scolded Red and walked past with that jug of cleaner, he would cower and hide. Even though he couldn't get the hang of the doggy door, he could certainly feel very, very bad every time the cleaning rags and chemicals came out.

Every parent knows how powerful shame can be in curbing behavior. As a mom of four kids, I'm ashamed (ha!) at the ways I have used a little light humiliation to change their behavior. When one of them scratched the car with his bike, I yelled way too long and hard about it, insisting to the child, "Look at that! See the damage you did?" When one of the kids has done a poor job of loading the dishwasher, I've described all the ways "a three-year-old could have done better." When our daughter listened to an inappropriate song, I had her listen to it with me to feel the shame of her mom hearing those words.

Ugh. I'm sorry—one million times, I'm sorry.

In the past decade, so much research has been done about the damaging effects of shame. As it turns out, this feeling is harder to shake than any other. Shame pierces your psyche in such deep ways that you will feel the trauma of it for decades to come. And it's never in a good way—because the message of shame is always, "You are not worthy, and don't you forget it."

This has been true for me. In fact, I'm so ashamed about stupid, reckless, selfish things I've done that I still feel the embarrassment of them right now—white-hot, fresh, and flowing through my veins as if it were boiling them. I'm like Red in that way. I, too, am walking around the house with a terrible mixture of shame and regret, looking for a corner to hide in.

Here's the worst news about shame: it's an effective tool to make someone feel guilty, but it rarely convinces them to actually change their behavior. It's such an all-encompassing emotion that it prompts the person to see themselves as wholly unworthy and powerless to change. This is the opposite of how I want my kids (or my dog, for that matter) to feel.

But, of course, shame is another one of those filters that your mind will construct because it can be such a bully. It says, "You, worthless person who is not capable of anything good, cannot be trusted. You are terrible and should live completely and fully in the knowledge that you are unworthy of love. Also, don't forget that most of the time, you have life really wrong. You never do enough."

Shame is a complete thought-filter. And the problem with filters is that they color absolutely everything. That's not what I want, and it's not what you want.

Here's what I wish I could tell my kids, myself, my dog, and you about past mistakes: you're forgiven. Jesus bought this forgiveness on the cross, and now Christ is in you. Paul preaches this truth in Romans 8:1, when he says, "There is therefore now no condemnation for those who are in Christ Jesus." Since Christ died for you, the Holy Spirit is doing a new thing in you. This sanctification means that the process of new life and a fresh outlook and opportunity are all right here.

What if, for today, you removed the shame goggles and lived the way John describes in 1 John 1:5–10? Live out this new life. We can "walk in the light" (v. 7) because of the blood of Jesus, which "cleanse[s] us from all unrighteousness" (v. 9).

The message of the Gospel, friends, is the Good News that Jesus took on the punishment for your sins. He made things right for you. As John describes in 1 John 1:5–10, you are no longer in the darkness.

You don't have to view the world from behind the couch, cowering because you're not perfect enough to get to heaven. The Spirit creates a clean heart in you and restores your joy. This life in the Spirit is how we are able to live fully loved, completely forgiven, and as a daughter of God.

For Today

1. Talk (or write) about what damage shame may have done to you. How do you feel when you're ashamed? How do Jesus' love and sacrifice free you from that terrible shame? What does that mean for you going forward?

2. Read Hebrews 12:12–16 as a prayer for spiritual strength and not to grow weary. Look especially at verses 12–14. Write what these words mean to you and the strength and love that you have through Jesus Christ.

3. For the last time, let yourself really feel the shame. Remember an incident that always makes white-hot shame wash over you, and experience it fully. Remember how it felt to be so embarrassed and to see yourself as totally unworthy. And then, look at the cross of Jesus Christ. Pray. Ask God to take away the sting of that shame and replace it with the joy of the Holy Spirit. He took it away from us when He laid our sins on Jesus and gave to us His perfect, spotless life in exchange. Next time you remember that shameful incident, think of God's promise in Romans 8:1 instead.

Challenge!

Today, write a letter to shame about the damage and pain it has caused you. Tell shame about how its toxic combination of pride and failure has caused you suffering. Be as specific as you need to be here. Next, write a second letter to yourself from Jesus, using the words of Hebrews 9:26; 1 John 1:9; 2 Corinthians 12:9–10. Tell about God's grace and how Jesus' love has changed your story.

Prayer

Dear Jesus, thank You for coming to earth and living and dying for me. Help me remember that because of Your perfect life and sacrifice, I am forgiven. Please, Lord, give me strength to see myself as the new creature I really am. Amen.

DAY 5

DRY, TIRED, THIRSTY, BROKEN BONES

All Scripture is breathed out by God and profitable for teaching, for reproof, for correction, and for training in righteousness. (2 Timothy 3:16)

Where do you stand on the sparkling water trend? Are you team "Give Me All the Water" or "Stop Paying for Lame Drinks"? Or maybe you're somewhere in the middle. In our house, three of us pretty much live to drink fizzy water with a little bit of blackberry or lime essence in it. There are also three very confused and mean people in our house who call our sparkling-water consumption an "addiction" and "ridiculous."

Clearly, I'm all for all the sparkling water all the time.

I love this stuff so much that it interferes with my life in significant ways—and I don't even care. Last night, we went to a dinner at a friend's house—one who is known for the tasty cocktails he makes but doesn't often have much sparkling water available. So I brought seven of my own. I drank them all before we came home. That didn't even feel excessive, compared to how many I drank the rest of the day.

My husband, Mike, bought me one of those carbonation machines so I could make our own water sparkle, which I do when I'm home and need a constant supply of fizziness in my life. So many bubbles, so little time.

Because children imitate what they see, two of my kids feel the same way about sparkling water. If you saw us loading the car for church, you might think we were headed to a day at the beach. We have a little cooler to keep the stash cool, and we take insulated travel mugs of water into the service so we look normal and are not cracking open cans of water.

I bet you think I'm going to say I'm ashamed that my love of strawberry-essence water is ruling my life and that's a problem. Not really. Because, actually, it's solving a different problem we had.

For years, we were dehydrated. I have allergies, and so do our two fizzy-water-loving kids. We are mouth breathers. Mouth breathing—in addition to living where it's hotter than the surface of the sun most days, plus being active and often outdoors—meant we needed way more hydration than we were getting.

As we got more active, we drank more and more soda, iced tea, juice, and sports drinks—but not as much water. One of our kids had constant headaches, and the other would feel tired until he drank a big glass of water. We hadn't even realized this was a problem until we developed a taste for the effervescent fruit-flavored stuff that was suddenly everywhere. My head cleared; my mouth wasn't as dry; I could even see better. I didn't know I needed it, but when I got the hydration my body was quietly craving, I felt like a different person.

That realization was so dramatic that I realized I was quietly desperate for another kind of hydration too.

My soul needs hydration. I may go for days feeling haggard, afraid, foggy, weary, isolated, pained, and with low-grade anger clouding my vision. What is this? What is the desperate sadness inside of me? Where is this longing coming from? How can I fix it?

Can I remind you of the powerful story of the dry bones in Ezekiel 37? On the land in front of Ezekiel, dry bones were spread out as the ultimate image of death and destruction. Then the Spirit (the Hebrew word here is *ruach*) spoke through Ezekiel, a prophet. With this breath, this *word*, the dry bones began to rattle with life. They were restored and full of flesh and functioning again. What had looked dead before was suddenly alive. Ezekiel's beautiful description of what happened to the dry bones (vv. 7–10) is so dramatic:

> So I prophesied as I was commanded. And as I prophesied, there was a sound, and behold, a rattling, and the bones came together, bone to its bone. And I looked, and behold, there were sinews on them, and flesh had come upon them, and skin had covered them. But there was no breath in them. Then He said to me, "Prophesy to the breath; prophesy, son of man, and say to the breath, Thus says the Lord GOD: Come from the four winds, O breath, and breathe on these slain, that they may live." So I prophesied as He commanded me, and the breath came into them, and they lived and stood on their feet, an exceedingly great army.

Here's the part of that prophesy that is so interesting to those of us who have been spiritually dehydrated: God showed Ezekiel something in the bones that wasn't there. The prophet even admitted that he couldn't picture these dried-out symbols of death as anything else (v. 3). God performed this miracle of covering them with flesh and ligaments so they were living, active bones again. God re-created the body—the one that looked as dead as a skeleton in the dried-out land.

When you're spiritually dehydrated, you don't quite know what's wrong, but a part of you knows you are not supposed to feel this harried, depleted, and afraid. That part cannot be filled with more money, success, or friends—or even sparkling water.

That part is crying out for the powerful Word of God. That is why Jesus said, "Whoever drinks of the water that I will give him will never be thirsty again. The water that I will give him will become in him a spring of water welling up to eternal life" (John 4:14).

This real nourishment, my friend, is what God provides for you every moment of every day.

For Today

1. Write (or talk) about how spiritual dehydration feels to you. When do you know that you're parched for the powerful Word of God?

2. Read Ezekiel 37:11–14, 26–27. What does God promise His people here? What about you—what do these words mean to you today?

3. Pray for your frazzled, weary soul. Ask God to give you and those you love His Spirit. Tell God how you need His hydrating and nourishing love right now to help you see His power and love in your life and to strengthen your faith in Him. Rest in the promise that He will fill you with exactly what you need.

Challenge!

Drink eight full glasses of water today. Indulge in sparkling water if that's what you like. With every glass, read a Bible verse and ask God to seal this message into your heart. Here are suggestions for verses: Psalm 143:6; Psalm 3:3–4; Romans 8:26; Ephesians 1:19–20; Jude 1:24; Hebrews 11:1; Galatians 2:20; Romans 15:13.

Pray

Heavenly Father, give me eyes of faith to know that You provide what I need. Please fill me with Your Spirit of love and faith. Help me to keep coming back to You, over and over, to renew and refresh me. Amen.

DAY 6

WILL THERE BE A TEST ON THIS?

The God of our Lord Jesus Christ, the Father of glory, may give you the Spirit of wisdom and of revelation in the knowledge of Him, having the eyes of your hearts enlightened, that you may know what is the hope to which He has called you. (Ephesians 1:17–18)

A couple of years ago, I went back to teaching.

I had taught before. It feels like a million years ago that I graduated from college and got my first job as a middle school and high school teacher at Lutheran South Academy in Houston. This was a long time ago—in the days covered with the fear about Y2K and the sadness over September 11. This was so long ago that most of my students didn't have cell phones. I was young and passionate and spent my after-school hours advising the yearbook staff and creating interesting lessons that I taught from overhead transparencies. (Yes, *so* long ago.)

Then, about twenty years ago, my first book was published, and I stayed home to write more and raise our kids.

For the next couple of decades, my roles were mom to our four kids and writer when they slept.

Our lives were full with babies and sports and travel and house projects. But I still missed teaching and the students, especially seniors. I love this moment in these kids' lives, right before they take the next step and leave childhood for college or a career. Over the past seventeen years that I've raised my own kids, I have understood more and more what a dramatic and bittersweet time senior year really is.

Then, a couple of years ago, Lutheran South offered me a job teaching seniors. I ran back into the classroom. For me, teaching is more a calling than a job. I could not wait to get back to it—the grading, the tough students, laughing with the kids, the school pride—all of it.

Something was different, though. In the past twenty years, students everywhere had changed. They had become very good at the internet and research through technology. Specifically, they had learned this lesson: to find the answer to any question, look somewhere else.

This was a problem because much of English class—especially for seniors, who are seventeen and eighteen years old—is about forming organic opinions about what to believe. One aspect that I love about teaching is hearing the (sometimes really out-there but oftentimes really insightful) opinions of my students. When we read *Hamlet*, for example, we debate it, and the students express what they believe about Horatio and whether or not it is a good play. Back in the day, we would put Hamlet on trial, and the kids would debate whether he was insane or faking it.

But these new students are not interested in class discussions. These kids are digital experts. They have always had the internet at their fingertips. Now, when we finish reading an act of the play, they may look up at me and wait for me to tell them what it means. When I ask them questions, they respond with zero comments, answers, or opinions. Their fingers itch to Google the answer.

"Come on," I tell them. "Just tell me what you think."

But they don't. Sharing an unresearched opinion doesn't make sense to them—googling the right answer does. I had hoped this literature would spark ideas, discussions, and debates, but my students are not for it. Their own opinions seem arbitrary and weak next to the authority of the SparkNotes website—or worse, the rambling blog of some random English teacher who has an agenda he wants kids to believe. To them, literature isn't something to be enjoyed—it's something to be researched and mastered.

What about you? Is this how you read the Bible?

Does it feel like a textbook, and you need to search for the right answer? Are you also a digital expert who likes the hunt for information? Do you get the sense that you're missing the overarching point of Scripture?

Or have you experienced the Bible differently? What about the Bible as inspiration? How about reading it as an epic saga of God's love? What about reading it every day for the immersive effect of understanding the spiritual food it is for us? What if God's Word wasn't meant as a research project for right answers but as a holy, inspired, light for our paths and a double-edged sword of truth?

That's totally what it is.

Paul tells us in 1 Corinthians 2:12–14 and 16 that the Bible is meant to be understood through the Holy Spirit, not the human mind. He goes on to say that if we read the Bible trying to make it all compute on an intellectual level, we are absolutely missing the point. Paul concludes this passage by reminding the new Christians that "we have the mind of Christ" (v. 17).

Wait, what? That's you and me he is talking about here. Because of Jesus' life and death, our souls are forever changed. When you read God's Word, you are immersed in it in the most important way possible. You are experiencing God's Word, which points to the love and sacrifice of His Son, Jesus, on your behalf so you don't have to fear death and hell. Your faith story and your personal history count. You bring with you your own unique experiences, perspectives, and history.

Bring this open heart to God's Word, dear friends. You are not reading because there will be a test on this later. You do not even have to know what every part means or how to apply it to your life. The answer of how to live isn't someplace else—it's right here. Inside God's Word, you will find the power of His love. You will know the testament of your Father's grace for you. His Word is life, and that is everything.

For Today

1. Imagine driving your car through a new area, and you are so afraid you'll get lost. You're not looking out the window at the beautiful sunset, the picturesque mountains, or the herd of cows grazing in the pasture. Instead, you're watching the map on your phone, worrying about making a wrong turn. Now, picture yourself driving through the streets of your beloved hometown or favorite vacation spot. How are these different? How can you engage with God's Word in both the second way and the first?

2. Read John 20:30–31; Hebrews 4:12–13. According to these verses, what is the purpose of the Bible?

3. Read Psalm 19:7–11 as a prayer:

> [7] The law of the LORD is perfect,
>   reviving the soul;
> the testimony of the LORD is sure,
>   making wise the simple;
> [8] the precepts of the LORD are right,
>   rejoicing the heart;
> the commandment of the LORD is pure,
>   enlightening the eyes;
> [9] the fear of the LORD is clean,
>   enduring forever;
> the rules of the LORD are true,
>   and righteous altogether.
>
> [10] More to be desired are they than gold,
>   even much fine gold;

> sweeter also than honey
>> and drippings of the honeycomb.
>
> [11] Moreover, by them is Your servant warned;
>> in keeping them there is great reward.

Challenge!

Try a new kind of fast today. For two hours, empty your life of all words. Avoid reading, listening to, texting, or saying anything. No internet at all today. Don't have the time and schedule to do this today? If not today, find a couple of hours in the next few days to try this fast. Record what happens when you take an intentional break from the constant stream of information that bombards you in a day. What do you notice is happening around you? What were you missing when you were immersed in information? Write it down, or share it with the group.

Pray

> **Holy Spirit, inspire me through the words of my Father. Give me peace, rest, encouragement, and wisdom. Lord, give me everything I need today from Your Word and this study. In the name of Jesus, I pray. Amen.**

THE MOLDY CHEESE WON'T KILL YOU

For this very reason, make every effort to supplement your faith with virtue, and virtue with knowledge, and knowledge with self-control, and self-control with stead-fastness, and steadfastness with godliness, and godliness with brotherly affection, and brotherly affection with love. (2 Peter 1:5-7)

For the past few years, a popular T-shirt slogan has been, "Be kind!" There are variations of the message, such as "Kindness matters!" and "In a world where you can be anything, be kind." This slogan is not only on T-shirts, but it's also on back-packs, water bottles, and bumper stickers. Kindness is suddenly everywhere.

And yet, it doesn't seem like there is kindness in our schools, neighborhoods, or churches. Kindness most certainly *does* matter, but many times it also feels extinct. As a mom and a teacher, I see the absence of this most often in how we parent. Let me say that more directly: our generation is teaching the next how to be mean and self-righteous.

It's time to give the next generation a new example—one of radical, deep, spiritual kindness. It's time to model the spiritual fruit of kindness we have through the Holy Spirit (Galatians 5:22).

Here's the problem we're facing: our generation has received the message that we have to keep our kids safe at all times. A generation of kids is being raised by parents who worship them and the idea of keeping them safe. Instead of trusting God to take care of these kids, we are taking all the responsibility. And we so often get it wrong.

We've lost the kindness. I'm not talking about T-shirt-slogan kindness; I mean the kind that comes from the Holy Spirit and is swathed in divine humbleness, gentleness, and patience. I'm talking about kindness that could change the world. I'm talking about the kindness that Peter describes in 2 Peter 1 when he tells about the exponential effect that goodness and love have in the world.

First, let's open our eyes to what this kindness really looks like.

We might start by easing up on protecting. Our kids are learning to be scared, and they will continue to learn that lesson if we keep trying to control their environment. When we teach children that the world is full of scary people, we are setting up a volatile relationship between them and the rest of society.

Recently, my daughters and I were at a meeting for a volunteer group with which we serve. The mom hosting the meeting prepared turkey sandwiches and arranged them on a plate in the kitchen. Another mom worried that the turkey had sat out for over an hour while we held our meeting. She warned her girls to stay away from the sandwiches, and she mentioned to the mom that it was not safe for us to eat the lunch meat.

No one ate the sandwiches. Ouch.

I wanted to hug this woman, who was trying to be a good host. On the way home, I talked to my girls about what had happened. We discussed how so much about the meeting had been about how to serve our community. And yet, none of us had shown real kindness to the hostess. Being safe had trumped raw, awkward, beautiful kindness.

My daughters admitted that the value they are taught most often is to be safe. We talked about how it is certainly a mom's responsibility to keep her children safe, but it is also so much more.

Our generation should show others how to live out the type of kindness that Jesus showed, to advocate for the truly marginalized, to listen with an open heart and mind, and to love those who need it the most. Kids cannot learn to do that if they are constantly afraid of the world. Their fear wins out over faith in such an ugly way.

Life in our corner of the suburbs is ruled by moms who call themselves "mama bears" and pride themselves on policing everything that involves their children. Examples sound like this:

"So, I emailed the principal and explained how the teacher is shaming my child when he reprimands her for being tardy in front of the whole class."

"When I heard that the gym teacher yelled at my child, I was at the school before the end of the day, informing her that she has no right to treat my baby like that."

"I stayed after practice and let the coach have it for making our kids stand out there in the rain."

The spiritual fruit of kindness is the opposite of this kind of self-righteousness. It is humbleness. It is sacrifice. It's not teaching others to repay yelling with yelling. It's the golden rule of treating others the way you want to be treated. It's the words of Leviticus 19:18 ("You shall love your neighbor as yourself") that Jesus referenced in Matthew 7:12 ("So whatever you wish that others would do to you, do also to them") and Luke 6:31 ("And as you wish that others would do to you, do so to them").

But most of all, kindness is grace.

Because here is the truth: we are all so flawed. Teachers lose their tempers. Coaches get frustrated with the less talented kids. The scout leader has a migraine and zero patience. That one mom simply forgot to invite your kid to the movie night. Lifeguards don't see it when the pool bully dunks your daughter. Whatever the circumstances, it's all sin, and it's in all of us.

You can't control how these other people react, but there is something you can do. Every single person in your path can receive your grace.

The teacher who wrongly accused your kid of talking during the math test? Just skip the angry voice mail. Your kid probably was talking at the wrong time, and a gentle discussion at home can fill in the blanks.

The losing basketball coach who doesn't do the drills you suggest? Instead of holding him after practice to tell him how to do his job, sit in the stands and cheer for every player on your daughter's team.

The kid who called your daughter a four-letter word at recess? Confronting her mom is probably not going to change much. In fact, you will be the punch line of that mom's joke. Four-letter words aren't a big deal in their house.

And the woman who is serving cheese with a bit of mold on the corner? She doesn't know, and she is just doing her best. Scrape off the moldy bit and eat the cheese. You won't die. More importantly, you will have taught the next generation a little about being a gracious guest, about the resilience of the immune system, and—most important—about being kind. You will have shown grace instead of more self-righteousness. Modeling this kindness to others changes them, and that can transform our whole culture.

True kindness comes from the Holy Spirit; it's something for which we are all hungry for more. We need this connection with one another. We need the flow of love that comes from real humility, modesty, and meekness.

When the world sees this fruit of the Spirit, it's inspiring. It really is. It reminds you of how Jesus lived. It shows the world something so different—the incredible grace of our Father.

It starts with each of us. Let's change the world by showing it how true, humble kindness looks. Even though this soft-heartedness begins at home, it's lived out in our communities.

The fruit of the Spirit is a response to the grace we receive from Christ's work for us and a gift that we received when we were baptized. Despite our sins, God loves each one of us so much. He takes perfect care of you, me, and all the children.

Let this inspired kindness flow to others so they see the love of our Father.

For Today

1. Where do you find kindness in your life? Where is it missing? Talk about this fruit of the Spirit. What would radical kindness inspire in your community? When have you seen this happen?

2. Read Colossians 1:11; Ephesians 4:2. In these verses, Paul encourages patience. How does patience (another fruit of the Spirit) go along with true kindness? Write (or talk) about that here.

3. This week, write in your prayer journal about a person with whom you struggle to show kindness. Ask the Holy Spirit to give you patience, peace, and self-control. Pray for divine kindness from God and to treat others the way you would like to be treated. Pray for this person every day and for his or her life to be filled with faith, love, joy, and goodness.

Challenge!

Kindness isn't an outward decision; it's a fruit of the Spirit that increases thanks to the Spirit's work in us through Word and Sacrament. For today, practice radical kindness to yourself by taking care of your spiritual life. Turn on your favorite hymn or worship music. Go outside and give your soul time to rest in God's creation. Ask a praying friend to pray for you today. Read your favorite Bible verse or passage.

Pray

Holy Spirit, work in my soul and fill me with Your goodness, patience, and kindness. Help me to love others and show them the fruit of my faith. Let me live like my Savior, Jesus. In His holy and precious name, I pray. Amen.

You Already Have Everything You Need

Jesus said to her, "Everyone who drinks of this water will be thirsty again, but whoever drinks of the water that I will give him will never be thirsty again. The water that I will give him will become in him a spring of water welling up to eternal life." (John 4:13–14)

What in the world causes you or me or anyone to buy hundreds of rolls of toilet paper? We do not have the immediate need, the space, or the organization to deal with all this toilet paper. (Current plan: stuffing them in the top shelf of the kids' closets, from where they will inevitably fall every time we need something from up there.)

When I take a quick glance at my own house, I see all the things I hoard: my favorite no-show socks that I fear no-show-ing in the dryer, twenty cartons of chicken broth (assuming I'm cooking for a small army), enough tea bags to wallpaper our house, and twenty-seven water bottles for the athletes in our house so they can always carry one (or six) of them to practice.

But my hoarding tendency is nothing compared to what happens to me emotionally when I'm around someone I admire, feel threatened by, or perceive as a competitor. In those situations, I'm not stockpiling paper goods; I'm trying to hoard something different. I want what she has. I want her life.

Maybe you can relate.

In my most insecure moments, I am a black-belt coveter. If your life looks easier than mine, I want it. If you're financially secure, I wish for your money. If I could, I would hoard your kids' good grades and their high SAT scores for my own. I would grab all of the extra hours you seem to have in your day and stuff them into mine. If I believed it were possible, I would clear the shelves and steal all of your sparkling joy and easy sense of humor and then also make a mad dash to get your hair that looks great in the humidity.

I tell you this because I'm pretty sure you feel the same way. The same scarcity instinct that makes you buy your favorite T-shirts in bulk also makes you feel like you need the better marriage that your sister has or the prettier house that belongs to your neighbor.

This coveting business has been a problem since the very beginning of human existence. However, at this particular moment in history, it's the worst it's ever been. Thank you, social media.

Suddenly, we have all these convenient platforms to compare ourselves to others incessantly. If you thought coveting was bad when Moses delivered the Ten Commandments, how about now, when you can easily compare the perfect life someone is cultivating online with the crummy one actually unfolding in your own messy kitchen?

Ugh. This hoarding and coveting feels like the worst kind of sin.

The older I get, the more I realize that jealousy is at the root of so much of the dysfunction in our lives. First, coveting is a giant exercise in ignoring the ways that God is already taking care of you. Second, it really is so damaging to relationships. If you want what she has, then you are scheming, planning, hoping, and designing a life of competition and hurt, instead of a life of support.

Do you know what I mean? Has this already been playing out in your life? Is the need for "more, more, more" damaging you too?

I can tell you the most important, soul-deep truth: you already have everything you will ever need. Period. End of story. It's all there. You can't buy or rent or steal or covet anything that will give you more of what you *truly* need.

How does that message land with you? Do you recognize the truth that God has already given you everything to take perfect care of you?

Listen to these powerful promises that Paul wrote to the Ephesians. (By the way, Paul wrote this letter when he was in prison—when he had nothing! No one-hundred-rolls-of-toilet-paper-but-not-enough-food and absolutely zero chance to stock up during a big sale.)

Paul prays for spiritual strength for the Ephesians:

> For this reason I bow my knees before the Father,
> from whom every family in heaven and on earth
> is named, that according to the riches of His glory
> He may grant you to be strengthened with power
> through His Spirit in your inner being, so that

> Christ may dwell in your hearts through faith—
> that you, being rooted and grounded in love, may
> have strength to comprehend with all the saints
> what is the breadth and length and height and
> depth, and to know the love of Christ that sur-
> passes knowledge, that you may be filled with
> all the fullness of God. Now to Him who is able
> to do far more abundantly than all that we ask
> or think, according to the power at work within
> us, to Him be glory in the church and in Christ
> Jesus throughout all generations, forever and ever.
> Amen. (Ephesians 3:14–21)

This passage is filled with so much truth about how the Holy Spirit provides you with everything you need. Take in these words and know deeply that the Spirit is strengthening you in your inner being. This knowledge is more intimate than head knowledge (v. 19); it is "rooted and grounded" in the love of Christ (v. 17).

Amid all this inspiring truth, verse 20 gives us the message we all need the most. God is able to do far more than we ask for or even think. He gives you everything you need, and then He gives the things you don't even realize you need. All of it. Abundance on top of abundance, and then even more abundance. These gifts are not more stuff crammed into your closets; this abundance is what you really need.

You have all the love you need. You have all the talent and energy and time you need to create what God put you here to create.

You have had what you need since the beginning; you will continue to have it; you will have it all for eternity.

For Today

1. What do you hoard? What triggers your jealousy when you see it in another person? What do you find yourself coveting over and over?

2. Read 2 Corinthians 9:8 several times. Each time you read this verse, think of something you feel you need right now. What do you hope to accomplish with all of these possessions? What feeling are you chasing by believing you need more? On the other hand, what are the good works that God equips you to do?

3. Ask God to bless you with the very gifts you need right now to equip you for the life He has given you. Pray for Him to give you the fruit of the Spirit: "Love, joy, peace, patience, kindness, goodness, faithfulness, gentleness, self-control" (Galatians 5:22–23).

Challenge!

You have finished the first week of your best spiritual life. My prayer is that you would understand God's love in a new way and that the Holy Spirit would nurture deeper faith in your life every day.

Resist the urge to hoard today. Look around your house and take an inventory of things you stockpile. List them, then write what triggers you to want so much of these things in your house. Turn this list into a journal entry about how this feeling of scarcity pokes at your deep insecurities. Write yourself a note about why you don't actually need so much extra stuff. Refer to your favorite words from Ephesians 3:14–21.

Pray

Thank You, Lord, for the gifts You give me through Your Spirit. Fill me with an abundance of Your love, joy, peace, patience, kindness, goodness, faithfulness, gentleness, and self-control. Amen.

PRAYER

INSPIRED IN PRAYER: INTRODUCTION

Likewise the Spirit helps us in our weakness. For we do not know what to pray for as we ought, but the Spirit Himself intercedes for us with groanings too deep for words. And He who searches hearts knows what is the mind of the Spirit, because the Spirit intercedes for the saints according to the will of God. And we know that for those who love God all things work together for good, for those who are called according to His purpose. (Romans 8:26–28)

We own a little cottage by the beach that we rent out during the summer. For several years now, Best of Times Beach House has been a hideaway for families who want to get away from the hustle of the suburbs. Actually, though, I get as much joy from sharing it as the families who vacation there do.

Over the years, we've had hundreds of families stay at our beach house, and I've learned a few lessons along the way.

First, almost every family brings sand toys and boogie boards to the house. They all arrive with brand-new shovels and buckets. And when they go home, they almost always leave the sand toys behind. As a result, we have a lifetime supply of these things. (Same with ice cream, by the way. And phone chargers. They're like reverse souvenirs that everyone forgets when they finish their vacation.)

Here's another thing I've learned about renting out our house. There is always one person who is responsible for planning the trip. It's usually the alpha female. She's the one who thinks through all the meals, what groceries they need to buy, which restaurants have the best reviews, and which one has a wheelchair ramp for Grandma.

While this mom is planning the trip, I hear from her often. Where's the best place for firewood? How can we deep-fry the fish my husband is planning to catch? Who can teach the kids to surf? Any suggestions for the best beach and time of day to take a family photo?

Then comes check-in day, and the family arrives at the beach house to begin their vacation. I almost always get a text when they arrive. "We are here and discovered that you have a drip-style coffee maker. We've only brought coffee pods, and I've already done the grocery shopping for the whole week. What are we supposed to do?"

It's not always about making coffee, but the tone of the text is always the same: mild panic. This woman, who has been solely responsible for all the details, realizes that one has slipped by her. And that makes her feel like everything is out of control.

I understand this because I'm that mom when our family travels to the mountains, or the lake, or the city. I'm the one who is spinning all the plates, thinking through schedules and budgets and the particular needs of every person in my family. I get why it's so jarring when you've come all that way and have made all those plans only to realize that the rental house has the wrong kind of coffee setup.

But here's what else I know will happen next—because it always does for our family and for those who rent Best of Times.

The family lugs their coolers, chairs, towels, and sand toys to the beach. They plop it all down, the kids run into the surf, and the mom cracks open the chair (and often her favorite drink) and collapses into it.

In a few moments, she notices the sound of the waves crashing, the salty smell of the air, the breeze off the Gulf, and the soft sand under her bare feet. Then, she looks up to see the pelicans soaring overhead in perfect formation.

All of this beauty and order and nature is happening here. Effortlessly. Without her needing to do anything. She sighs deeply and feels the profound peace that comes with witnessing something absolutely delightful—something that she is not in charge of and that she couldn't control even if she wanted to.

About this time, I will call to ask about the coffee situation. Everything has changed. That minor panic at check-in is gone. She is sitting in the middle of miraculous beauty. Something deeper than words has righted itself when she is there, with those she loves, amid God's wonderful creation.

"The coffee?" she'll say. "Oh, we'll figure it out. It's totally fine. By the way, we love your house so much."

She doesn't mean she loves our house. It's not the house that has given her this moment that she has needed so desperately. She needed the reminder that God is in control and that He is very good at it.

In truth, all of us want and need God to be in control. Prayer is all about this need. Prayer is the holy invitation to share our greatest fears, plans, sins, hopes, needs, and praises with the Creator of the universe.

It is our privilege to share all of these thoughts with God. Paul mentions these spiritual groanings, too deep for words, in Romans 8:26. These prayers are not for what we want; they are for what we need. God always (always!) gives us what we need. He always works all things together for good for those who love Him, whether we ask Him to or not. When we pray, the Holy Spirit is interceding for your deeper needs—peace, love, eternal security, and faith. Just wow. This is a miracle, and it is part of living an inspired life: enjoying the perfect care of your heavenly Father, the deep love of Jesus, and the power of the Holy Spirit.

For Today

1. Talk (or write) about what groanings you believe you
    have, the ones that are too deep for words. What has
    been your experience with prayer? Share stories of
    how God has answered your prayers, both dramati-
    cally and more mundanely.

2. Read Luke 11:10–13. Write the message of this pas-
    sage in your own words here. What are the good
    things God gives us?

3. Read 1 Thessalonians 5:16–18. Ask the Holy Spirit to
    inspire the things mentioned in this passage in your
    heart this week (praying without ceasing; rejoicing
    always; giving thanks in all circumstances; the will
    of God). Pray for protection against spiritual attacks
    from the enemy. Ask in Jesus' name for gifts that
    your Father knows will bless you.

This Week

Prepare for a week drenched in prayer. Spend this week praying on your knees, in the shower, in the car, as you fall asleep,
and when you wake up. Pray as you breathe—in and out, in
and out.

Pray

**Heavenly Father, give me the miracle of faith so I
can better see the ways You are taking care of me.
In the name of Jesus, I pray. Amen.**

THE KITTEN STORY

Pray then like this: "Our Father in heaven, hallowed be Your name. Your kingdom come, Your will be done, on earth as it is in heaven. Give us this day our daily bread, and forgive us our debts, as we also have forgiven our debtors. And lead us not into temptation, but deliver us from evil." (Matthew 6:9-13)

A few weeks ago, my daughters and I went to volunteer with a charity we serve, a philanthropy that finds homes for abandoned kittens.

A local pet store lets this little rescue group keep their cages in the corner of their store. Our job as volunteers is to feed the kittens, clean out their cages, and play with them. My girls like this job because the kittens are very cute little balls of fur—and, really, who doesn't like cuddling kittens?

We do this work right before the pet store closes so the kittens have clean litter, fresh food, and water for the night. On that evening, we were just finishing up when a couple came through the door and to the kitten kennels.

Sometimes, when people see us playing with the kittens, they ask if they're up for adoption and we chat with them about the rescue group. This couple knew what they wanted, though. They explained that they had been by twice to love on this tiny gray-and-white kitten. They were so excited to take it home that very night.

I explained that we weren't allowed to adopt out the kittens; we were cage-cleaner-level volunteers. Pet adoption requires an application and fees, and we didn't have the authority for any of that.

But the young girl was snuggling and kissing the cat, and it was clear that she really, really wanted it. I pulled out my phone and texted Sarah, the volunteer in charge of adoptions, and asked if she could come to the pet store quickly and process their application. She texted back that she was in a meeting and wouldn't be there for another thirty minutes.

"I'm so sorry," I told the couple. "There's no way. The pet store needs to close, and we don't have an application for you to fill out."

But the couple didn't hear me. The kitten had snuggled her way up the young woman's hoodie and was purring and pawing. This little cat was sealing the deal. On top of that, the girl was giving her boyfriend *the look* that young men everywhere know—the one that says, "This is what I need for my happiness, and you had better figure this out."

The boyfriend started pacing. "Come on," he told her. "Let's come back tomorrow. They need to leave. We'll get some dinner instead. I'm hungry."

Just then, the owner of the pet store came over and told us they were closing. We had five minutes to get the kittens in their kennels so they could lock the doors. We all looked at the girl and the kitten—who were both staring us down. Meanwhile, the boyfriend was breathing out frustrated sighs.

"So sorry," I said. "You'll have to come back tomorrow to get the kitten. It's just not going to work tonight."

She was angry, and the boyfriend was glaring at her. "Tomorrow won't work," she said. "I have to work the next five days, and I can't make it over here. It has to be tonight. The store will stay open later. Someone will be here for a long time closing up. We're not buying anything, anyway. Sarah could be here in thirty minutes."

The pet store employee said that she really needed to leave. All of us could see that this kitten wasn't going home with this young woman tonight—all of us except her.

I couldn't help but notice how this girl needed the cat so desperately that it was clear it wasn't about the cat at all. Her boyfriend snapped at her, stormed out, and went to wait in the car. She looked like she was going to cry.

That was last month, and I've thought about that woman so many times since then because her need for that kitten was a force that was heavy, scrappy, fierce, and troubling.

It's also something I totally recognize in myself.

I know, so well, the desperation to demand something from life that feels key to my survival or my happiness. Over the decades, I have desperately needed many things. It has been friends. To feel important. A husband, babies, the right career opportunities. Really, though, what I have always had is this grinding desire to be secure, accepted, and loved.

How many prayers have I cried out to God that were for a complicated situation to go my way? Or for an awkward situation to be resolved quickly? Or for more (more! more!) money, or more people who like me, or better health or kindness or patience?

And, of course, I've prayed for healing for those I love, for the problems haunting our world or family, and for those who don't know God to have faith. I have probably even prayed for a kitten in all my years of telling God what I really, really need.

You know what I mean, friend, because you've also felt a clawing, desperate excitement when the thing you need is *right there*, and if God would grant your wish to make it all work out, you would finally have it. The missing piece.

The missing peace.

Here's the thing. You also surely know that you don't always go home with the kitten. Sometimes you do, but other times, you don't get the miracle or thing you've wanted so badly. At the time, this feels like a bust because you were so sure of what you were asking God. Save our home. Heal our child. Give us our marriage back. Fill our home with love. But it doesn't play out the way you wanted.

If you're like me, this makes you cynical. If God loved you, wouldn't you get your miracle? The thing you need and were so obedient to ask for was clearly the good and righteous next turn in your life. What kind of attention-deficit God doesn't pay close enough attention to see that this is where your story was headed all along? Has He not been focused enough on you? Have you been praying to a cruel God? What about all those verses in the Old Testament about God punishing people and even asking Abraham to sacrifice his only child? This God has the wrong story for you. If God really loved you, you would have what your human heart wants.

Fortunately, that's not what prayer is at all. We may not always get what we want, but God promises to give us what we need. I don't always get the kitten I want at the moment I think I need it, but with every prayer, I do get the missing peace—the confidence that God has a better plan, a better way that I really need.

God gives us what we really need—His love, grace, mercy, and peace. They come with the knowledge that He has everything under control and will work out everything for our good. Our sovereign God loves us in the most generous and gracious way imaginable. Our loving Father sent His Son to die for our sins and always provides the better way. This is the Holy Spirit that draws us in and comforts us with that peace we can't even describe but that we know for sure is ours. He gives us the faith to trust that He is present for every breath, even through the grief, the fear, the scarcity, and the pain.

In fact, He is present *especially* through all of those trials. I see you, dear woman, who has dealt with all of these, and I can assure you that Jesus is real and so is His love for you. Every moment, every breath, every day, He is the Savior you need and that you have.

Forever and ever, for all of eternity, God is with you.

And *that* is what you really do need.

For Today

1. Look at your life right now and pick out areas where you are striving for love, security, courage, meaning, and acceptance. What do you find yourself doing when you're looking for meaning in life? What warning signs do you recognize when your soul is hungry for nourishment? Talk or write about how you feel when you're filled with God's peace and you feel the deep belonging of living as His daughter.

2. Read Psalm 1. What does life in the Spirit look like for you? What habits do you practice when you are "planted by streams of water" (v. 3)? What fruit do you produce? What habits are you practicing when you "are like chaff that the wind drives away" (v. 4)?

3. Read Philippians 4:4–9 as a prayer. Take deep breaths and read Paul's words about what life in the Spirit looks like over and over again. Ask God to be the God of peace in your heart so that you may be anchored to Him now and always.

Challenge!

Read the words to "Holy Spirit, Light Divine" (*LSB* 496):

Holy Spirit, light divine,
Shine upon this heart of mine;
Chase the shades of night away,
Turn the darkness into day.

Let me see my Savior's face,
Let me all His beauties trace;

Show those glorious truths to me
Which are only known to Thee.

Holy Spirit, pow'r divine,
Cleanse this guilty heart of mine;
In Thy mercy pity me,
From sin's bondage set me free.

Holy Spirit, joy divine,
Cheer this saddened heart of mine;
Yield a sacred, settled peace,
Let it grow and still increase.

Holy Spirit, all divine,
Dwell within this heart of mine;
Cast down ev'ry idol throne,
Reign supreme, and reign alone.

Talk about the text of this hymn with a trusted faith mentor. Share which words strike you as especially beautiful descriptions of the Holy Spirit's work in your life through prayer. Tell him or her how the phrase "Show those glorious truths to me" in stanza 2 could be a response to something for which you are asking God right now.

Pray

Lord Jesus, give me what I need—more faith, more forgiveness, more love. Please bless me with the joy, the security, the delight, and the life that I need right now. In Your holy name, I pray. Amen.

HOW YOU DRAW A HOUSE (IS HOW YOU DO ANYTHING)

In the beginning, God created the heavens and the earth. The earth was without form and void, and darkness was over the face of the deep. And the Spirit of God was hovering over the face of the waters. (Genesis 1:1–2)

Go get a pen or pencil.

Set a timer for five minutes. The one on your phone is fine to use.

Now, draw a picture of a house. No skipping this part—even if the pen is all the way on the other side of the room or you don't feel like drawing a house.

You might not want to draw anything because there's a little bit of fear here. Maybe you're convinced you're pretty terrible at drawing. Maybe someone once criticized your drawing skills, or maybe you've learned to compare it to what a real sketch of a house should be. And once you start thinking about that, you might not want to waste the time with the little doodle that you can make.

But ignore all of that, and let your pen move across the paper.

For five minutes, really work on that picture. Draw the very best house you can. Try not to hesitate. Come on—put some thought and detail into it. Can you see into the windows? Is there a tree? What do the branches look like? Does the front door have a knob?

When time is up, look at your picture. What do you see there? Are you a little proud of how it turned out? Are you kind of embarrassed? Is there a second voice—one in your mind—that's critiquing your design and listing everything that's not perfect about the sketch? Did you feel the absence of that voice when you had a thing to make? Did the creative part of you remember old exhilaration from when you were a kid—the freedom to create something without worrying about wasting time, or what you would do with it, or what other people would say about it, or what a good or bad drawing meant about who you are?

Was there also this small part of you—the creating, exploring, curious part—that loved playing around with an idea and trying to make this picture into something else—to just keep creating? Did it feel thrilling or peaceful to turn off your critical brain for a few minutes and just make something?

Here's what I think—the way you felt while sketching that house is the way you feel about everything. If you're cynical about creating something new—even a few minutes to draw a little picture—your brain might be in the habit of shutting down the freedom to spend time and energy on it. For you right now, everything needs to stay on a schedule, the strict timetable of work, accomplishing, and succeeding. If it's not productive, then it's not worth your energy.

This often points to perfectionism in your life.

However, if you were curious about what you could make with this paper and this pen, you are likely open to the thrill of creating. You enjoy welcoming something new—even if imperfect and unformed—into your day. You will mess up, but the process of trying, failing, adding, and revising is the point. What if you add another door? Or a side porch? What is peeking out of the windows? Is that an apple tree in the front yard? Where did that little terrace come from? Huh. That's interesting. What else can I make?

Humans are creators. God has given all of us, His favorite creation, this wonderful gift of creativity. This gift pushes us to innovate, improve, beautify, and solve. This gift is mind-blowing. We get to be part of the process of making the world better through art and invention.

Stretching back through the history of composers, artists, and builders in the Bible, humans have been making new things for generations. Even while we suffer through war, poverty, and pandemics, we keep improving, embellishing, and inventing. We develop things we need—devices that make our lives easier—and we also create absolutely gorgeous art, just for the fun of it. The history of how something is created is filled with wonder and mystery. The ability to create is a gift from God, and it is our pleasure to make things that glorify Him.

Moreover, the act of making has so much to teach us.

In this process there is curiosity, then failure, then more wonder, then another attempt, then a loss of control, more attempts, and more piecing things together until you have made something new (something fantastic!) that is an expression of your imagination.

You can decorate your house, compose a breathtaking hymn, or write a little phrase to express exactly how the moon looks from the top of a mountain. The process is the same over and over, and it is filled with a transformation of one thing to another. A thought to a poem, a vision to a painting, lumber to a bookcase, pictures to tell a story—a transformation of this into that.

But it's more than that. The creative process reflects exactly what God is doing in your life all the time: new creation, making something that wasn't there, forgiveness where there was bitterness, peace where there had only been anxiety. Most importantly, the creative process brings spiritual transformation.

In the creative process, we see the mystery of what it means to live as a Christian. The Holy Spirit uses the Word and Sacraments to do the work of giving and sustaining our faith in the forgiveness Jesus offers. This is sanctification.

Can you see this transformation as the end to doubt, cynicism, self-hatred, and an obsession with perfection? That transformation is what you have wanted all along.

When you forget about God's grace for you, you might find yourself falling into all those terrible habits. You convince yourself that your salvation requires following rules, doing things exactly right, and never venturing into unknown territory. You believe that all the pressure is on you to be perfect. You forget about God's deep love and Christ's absolute perfection in your place.

You might see this same process when you do something creative. You see your own limitations. You keep trying and giving yourself second chances. And in the middle of it—the transformation of this old thing into this new one—you are humbled and then show yourself some grace. You face the truth that you are not in control of the end product. You give up your love of perfectionism and look for the grace instead.

The overwhelming Good News of Jesus' death on the cross is that the story does not end in sin and death. Instead, there is an eternal abundance of love, grace, peace, second chances, joy, forgiveness, and new life.

Moreover, the story does not end there. The Spirit that raised Jesus from the dead lives in you (Romans 8:11) and continues to work in you. This never-ending creation of new life in Christ is the process of a million second chances. You won't get stuck in what didn't work because God is doing a new thing in you. No more fear. No more stupid perfectionism on your shoulders.

What do you believe about the work of the Holy Spirit in your life? Do you know that the Spirit is dynamic and can create faith where there was none? Are you open to this miracle of your Baptism—or are you stuck in your unbelief?

Through His Word and Sacraments, God's Spirit is doing work full of wonder and mystery in your life all the time. Stay open to the powerful creation happening in you right now. Recognize the power of the Holy Spirit to heal your soul and empower your actions with love.

The mysterious difference between Christians and the rest of the world is that we believe in the divine creation of faith and forgiveness, and we trust God to electrify our souls with it. We trust that the impossible happens over and over every day. Over and over.

Embrace this process, live it, and celebrate it in your life.

For Today

1. Tell the group (or write on this page) about your attitude toward the creative process. How does grace play a part in this? Do you find the creative process to be comforting or terrifying? Why? What blocks do you have against creating?

2. Read Psalm 104. Read the whole psalm, but pay special attention to verse 30. Ask God to guide you to His Word for understanding about the Holy Spirit. Consider God's power to create and sustain the universe. Thank Him for the Holy Spirit, which gives you new life, renewal, spiritual nourishment, and transformation.

3. Write a prayer to God, the Creator and Sustainer of the universe. Ask Him to help You see the creative work He is doing. Confess areas in your life in which you are stuck and inflexible to the dynamic Spirit. Ask God to fill those places with faith and forgiveness.

Challenge!

Continue working on your drawing. Spend the next thirty minutes making that house into something even more—a mansion, a castle, or a resort. If you are feeling really bold, you can paint it or color it with markers or colored pencils. You can even frame it. In any case, put your drawing in a place where you can see it.

Yes, you will mess up. You might have to erase. You may kind of hate what you create. Hang it up anyway. Let it be a reminder of the process of transformation that God the Holy Spirit is working in your soul all the time. Something that didn't exist before is there now. Through His forgiveness, our God can erase our past mistakes and flaws as He continues His work in us. Redemption—over and over again.

Pray

Creator, Father, Lord, thank You for Your beautiful creation. Make something new in me. Send Your Spirit to transform my life. In Your Son's name, I pray. Amen.

TRAUMA AND NEW LIFE

If you love Me, you will keep My commandments. And I will ask the Father, and He will give you another Helper, to be with you forever, even the Spirit of truth, whom the world cannot receive, because it neither sees Him nor knows Him. You know Him, for He dwells with you and will be in you. (John 14:15–17)

Here's an interesting definition of trauma I heard recently: trauma is when an event redefines your life view.

This tracks with the trauma I've been through and watched people I love endure. We can probably all agree that no single year has caused as much national trauma as 2020.

What was 2020 like for you? Did you feel as if you were on a roller coaster of trauma and recovery, then new trauma would strike? COVID-19 was enough, but then there was civil unrest, crazy weather affecting so many people, and the collapse of our economy. So much trauma.

When we look back at the most dramatic parts of 2020, it's unbelievable how quickly our brains work to normalize it. You've never worn a face mask before, and now you and your children have to wear one all the time? Fine. You're active in a vibrant congregation and a regular part of the church community, and then for the next six months or even a year, all you can do is watch the worship service online. Is that fine? Our country is fighting all the time, on social media and the news, in our government and our families. Is that fine?

It's not fine. Life isn't supposed to be this way. And when it is this way, we're not supposed to be fine with it.

Here's the deal: I don't think any of us are actually really *fine* with the recent trauma and fallout. Our minds are spinning at how our world changed, but our minds don't like to spin for long. The human mind likes to make connections and draw conclusions and force the chaos into a shape and place that makes sense. We'll do anything to explain away the confusion and get back to fine.

Here are some examples you might know too: a friend of mine complains about her husband all the time. She tells me about her simmering anger about doing all the work. She gripes about how he exaggerates stories to look good and how her resentment spills over into their whole lives. They are low-grade mad at each other all the time. And then she also says she is "fine."

Another friend has a son who has made bad choices and wrecked so much of their lives. My dear friend has structured her life around the battles and the brokenness in this relationship. Her life was absolutely not supposed to go this way. But when we talk about it, she says it's "fine."

Why? I think we've gotten the idea that good Christians find contentment in any circumstance. But that's not exactly true.

These women are hurting so badly. When I talk to them about their situations, I hear their pain and outrage. When they verbally process it, the truth spills out that they are not fine. They are aching with sadness and outrage. They are trying to make sure their family looks normal. We are all working so hard to convince ourselves and everyone else that everything is fine.

I've shared this realization with my friends, and I share it with you too.

Christ teaches a different reality than your brain, which wants to make everything fine. You are upheld by the strongest, most holy, loving, powerful force imaginable—the Holy Spirit. He gives you abundant gifts of kindness, joy, peace, love, patience, gentleness, and self-control. His gifts help you deal with pain, outrage, and disappointment. This world is chaotic and sad and heartbreaking and painful. But because of Jesus, the chaos of this world will not remain forever. Christ will come and make everything perfect. That's a promise.

That's not normalizing pain. That's something so different and more powerful.

Jesus talked about this different kind of living when He showed the Pharisees that they were cleaning the outside of the cups and calling them clean (Matthew 23:25–26). They wanted control. They wanted the appearance. They wanted to fit in with what an outwardly good person should do. They wanted everything to be *fine*.

Jesus was pointing out that this is not fine. Their rules couldn't hide their sinful hearts and minds from God's eyes. Trying to control what showed on the outside was not going to give them the peace they needed. Denying the pain doesn't erase it. Instead, Jesus invited them to see their imperfection for what it was: more complete than they could imagine and also not the whole story.

The Pharisees' reaction to Jesus is all tied up in weird and sad attempts to control. We see it in ourselves today too. When tragedy strikes, we will try anything to keep the status quo, to keep being fine, fine, fine. But the Holy Spirit is not in the business of fine.

Oh, dear friend. *This* deeper reality is what trauma pokes at. The Holy Spirit works through the trauma. The Helper and Comforter is there to strengthen you, to empower you, and to give you the faith you need. Faith guides us to be vulnerable—to admit weakness, failure, and hopelessness. God is equipping you to handle the new reality with eyes wide open. You can look at what's broken with total honesty and say just how tragic it is. And then you can find security in what God is giving you.

Mercy. Forgiveness. Love. Eternity. They are still there. They always were and always will be. They are available because Jesus died for you and sent you the Holy Spirit.

For Today

1. Think or talk about one trauma you have survived. Name it. Talk or write about the destruction it forced into your life. Consider how it blew up your world. And yet—you're here, reading this book, thinking how you can weave more of God's perspective into the roller coaster that is your life. How has the Holy Spirit given you new perspective on the tragedies in your life? How has His love felt especially empowering after trauma? How has your Baptism and identity as God's daughter changed *everything*?

2. Read John 15:26. What does Jesus call the Holy Spirit in this verse? Based on your unique life, what is the deepest truth you have discovered about the Holy Spirit? How does that truth remain, even when everything else fails?

3. Even today, some small (or large) trauma may happen to you or someone you love. Pray or write in your prayer journal and ask God to send the Helper to give faith, joy, and love to this person who needs deep spiritual nourishment.

Challenge!

Name one system, relationship, or role in your life that has recently experienced trauma. Write it on a sheet of paper, and then write for ten minutes about the new reality this event brought into your life. Are you still following an old system even though life has drastically changed? Are you still treating a relationship like it was, even though you know it is radically different now? Take the most authentic and truthful next step here. Have the honest conversation you know you should. Pray that God strengthens you to change a bad habit. Take your weary soul outdoors, play worship music, and soak up the goodness of God's Word and promises and His perfect love.

Pray

Dear God, seal Your truth deep in my soul. Let me see Your care and protection, even when the world lets me down—especially when the world lets me down. Give me faith to rely on You every day. In Jesus' name, I pray. Amen.

DAY 13

A MORE EXCELLENT WAY TO LIVE

And let us consider how to stir up one another to love and good works, not neglecting to meet together, as is the habit of some, but encouraging one another, and all the more as you see the Day drawing near. (Hebrews 10:24-25)

As I write this, it's a few days before the 2020 presidential election, and our nation is torn as never before. When you read this, you will know the outcome of that election. Are cities still ravaged by protests? Is social media still a battlefield of rage and opinions? Has the passion and hate bubbled over into something awful, or have we found a way through it?

My hope is that a unifying voice has spoken up and led everyone back to the original plan—the plan to love one another. Maybe after this hard, hard election, we will have learned some lessons and have stopped digging trenches of pride and hatred. Come, Lord Jesus. Unify us to work together to help the vulnerable and love the unlovable.

My guess is that no matter when you're reading this, we are all still behaving pretty badly. We attach ourselves so much to our specific stories, our unique backgrounds, and our personal preferences. We are so filled with deep loyalty to long-held identities that we are not able to see the work of the Spirit.

This problem stretches all the way back to Paul's First Letter to the Corinthians. In chapter 12, he wrote that the Body of Christ has one Spirit but several different roles.

Paul wrote about spiritual gifts here, teaching about the division that comes from ego. The image of an eye rejecting the hand (v. 21) seems like a simple Sunday School illustration of why each of us should know that we're important to God. But that's not the only truth here. Paul's lesson is also about how we are way too good at celebrating our own opinions and very bad at being open to change, fellowship, and love. Each of us in the Body of Christ is focused too much on who we are individually and not enough on what we can do together.

My sons love the Astros, our hometown baseball team, and cannot stand the Dodgers or their fans. When we talk about this, they agree that they like the local team because everyone around them is wearing Correa jerseys and talking about how José Altuve lives right here in our city and shops at the same HEB market we do. They've gone to Astros games and cheered for the players in orange, just like I did forty years ago. Does that really mean the Astros are the better team? Isn't that also true for Dodgers fans who live in Los Angeles?

This same ridiculous mentality that "my way is better because it's my way" plays out in American politics and in destructive racial hatred. Your story is different, and your gifts are different—but if we are all living in the Holy Spirit, then we are all part of one Body.

Paul wrote in 1 Corinthians 12:13, "For in one Spirit we were all baptized into one body—Jews or Greeks, slaves or free—and all were made to drink of one Spirit." He wrote to groups who were dramatically, violently opposed to one another in every single way. Jews and Greeks were pressured for generations to live absolutely separately. Yet Paul was telling them that the Spirit directing their lives was the same Holy Spirit directing their enemy's lives. And, as he went on to say, that means we are all called to the more excellent way of love. If you're stuck hating the way *they* do it, then you are part of the division, part of the problem, and not working with the Body of Christ.

And so when you scroll through social media and see your Republican friends and your Democrat friends arguing about how we should help the most vulnerable in our society, you can see that they are coming at the same issue but from different perspectives. Sometimes they come from radically different perspectives—and then they dig their heels deeper into the sinking sand on their side.

But what about Paul's command in verse 31? He tells us to "earnestly desire the higher gifts. And will show you a still more excellent way."

What does that more excellent way look like? Love. The whole next chapter, 1 Corinthians 13, is about how to live together in love. Oh, wow. This message is beautiful. This unifying voice is what we need right now. We often hear Paul's words at weddings, but he wrote them to show us all how to treat others who are different than us. That includes not living in your own pride about how your specific perspective and opinion are right—as "a noisy gong or a clanging cymbal" (v. 1), which are the very most annoying noises—but to be patient and kind instead of arrogant or rude.

This unifying wisdom is what we all need to hear and we all need to show. Stop generating division and arrogance because these are not a reflection of Christ. It is hurting other people; it is hurting you. Those are childish ways. You are different now. Don't you see that all this information and wisdom is nothing if you don't have love? This means listening to others who are different than you. It means showing a country that is so buried in ego and anger what humbleness and peace look like.

This soul-deep softening doesn't mean gathering with your like-minded friends to complain about the other side. It means serving those who see the world differently than you do. Politicians yelling at one another is not love. Facebook rants are not love. Staying at home, safe with your opinions, is not love.

As Christians, we are one in the Spirit, and that means we act like it. For our family, this means serving at the food bank alongside others from drastically different backgrounds. It means listening to our friends who have seen oppression we can't understand. It means continually praying for humble hearts so we will not be angry, rude, irritable, or resentful (1 Corinthians 13:5). Mostly, it means living in the faith and hope of the Spirit so that we are not tempted to hide in our own bunkers of fear.

Even more than the faith and hope, though, my prayer for each and every Christian in the United States and beyond is love. Let us show the love we have through the Holy Spirit to one another. Let us live out Acts 2:4–6 and allow the Holy Spirit to work in our hearts to really understand one another. Because Paul is clear in 1 Corinthians 13:13 that love is our greatest calling.

Begin every day with this Spirit in you, not only to love those who think like you but also to love those who do not. Love those who pick fights. Love those who need lots and lots of grace. Love those who show you lots and lots of grace.

This is the more excellent way.

For Today

1. What political debates ignite your anger and fear? What temptation do you face to feel self-righteous and cruel? Talk about a recent time when you've found yourself arrogant toward another group. Do you think our country is more divided than a year ago? Why or why not? What hope do we have?

2. Read Ephesians 1:16–21. This is it, dear friends. This is our calling. The Father of all glory has given you, me, and Christians everywhere the Holy Spirit of wisdom and revelation. Our eyes are enlightened! We know hope! Our perspective is changed. We have love, and our calling is to act in that love. What does that look like in your life today? How does your specific story need the Spirit's love, and how can you show that?

3. Pray specifically about the pride that's in your heart. Ask the Holy Spirit to replace pride with love that never ends, never envies, never boasts, is never arrogant or rude, and never insists on its own way.

Challenge!

Today, give your love arms and legs and go serve the most vulnerable in your community. Your local food bank needs hands to serve the hungry. You know a sister in Christ who needs prayer and maybe a good meal dropped off on her porch. Someone in your family needs the forgiveness and grace that comes through Christ as well as a phone call to talk about his or her day. Go out, servants of God. Go with the Holy Spirit, in the name of Jesus, and show the world the more excellent way of love. Serve together to show the world the love of our heavenly Father.

Pray

Father, send the Holy Spirit to come upon us and infuse us with Your love. Give us a new perspective to see unity instead of division and humbleness instead of ego. Help us love one another well. In the name of our holy and precious Savior, I pray. Amen.

Iridescent and Deadly Tentacles of Control

But Jesus looked at them and said, "With man this is impossible, but with God all things are possible." *(Matthew 19:26)*

I grew up in Galveston, Texas, a small barrier island on the coast of Texas. As a BOI (born on island), I spent many weekends in the waves and lying on the shore. The beach is my happy place—but I also know its dangers.

Choppy, crashing waves are fun if you surf, but they can produce a dangerous undertow that will pull you far from the spot on the shore where you dumped your towel and flip-flops. My husband and kids love the sport of kayak fishing, but if they don't bring along lots of water and sunscreen, they return with headaches and terrible sunburns. In Galveston, our dunes are small, grassy cliffs that protect the island from the sea—a perfect habitat for rattlesnakes. Every summer, a curious dog is bitten when it heads into the dunes to investigate what that strange rattling sound is.

And then, there's the Portuguese man-of-war. These beautiful blue sea creatures look like regular jellyfish—but they are a special kind of creature (a hydrozoan) that is so much crueler. In Hawaii, the natives call these strange, stunning animals "the floating terror" because their sting is so painful.

If you were walking along the beach with me in the late summer, you would see, between the shells and clumps of seaweed, iridescent blobs that you'll need to step over. Their gas-filled bodies are about the size of a two-liter bottle, but their tentacles are the real scientific wonder. They are usually about six feet long and a stunning combination of purple, teal, bright green, and pinkish tendrils. Kids always want to pick them up because of their candy-like look. Even their scientific name sounds fun: *zooids*.

But in fact, the wondrous tentacles are terrible. These creatures look for prey and wrap their poisonous arms around anything that gets too close. Their sting leaves painful welts that islanders call "whip burns."

From Florida to France, these terrible critters wreak havoc on so many vacation plans. If you step into a coastal emergency room during the summer, the waiting room will have a few victims, crying out in pain from the poisoned welts. When a man-of-war wraps its tentacles around you, it takes vinegar, warm salt water, and ice for them to release you. The man-of-war uses its poison to paralyze small fish so it can eat them—and this same poison is released on a human calf or arm.

The other day while down on Galveston Island, I went for a long walk on my favorite stretch of beach. It was late summer—just when these pests usually float up from the

Caribbean and into our Gulf of Mexico, so I was looking out for them.

I was also worrying about everything—COVID. The failing economy. My twins, who were navigating the impossible social drama of middle school. Our oldest daughter, who was taking the PSAT that week. The strange pain below my ear that was either a growing cavity or brain cancer. All the plates my husband has to keep spinning in his job. My mom's autoimmune disease, which has disabled her and keeps progressing. My dad's faulty heart. My mind was spiraling with the horrible realization that I had zero control over any of this. Not really.

I so badly wanted to help all of these people. I still do, even as I write this. I want to control all these situations. I want to help, help, help.

But here's what I'm also learning. Sometimes, giving help is just the sunny side of being in control.

What I've discovered is that this instinct to control is as poisonous to my soul as the tentacles of the man-of-war are to my flesh.

You have discovered this too, dear friend. Those tentacles of control are at the root of so much of your sin. The long, slimy appendages wrap themselves around your mind and soul and give you the idea that you can take care of anything. Just worry about it a little more. Just believe it's up to you and that you can control anything.

Those tentacles are causing so much pain in your life. Control is a deadly illusion. Even though this beautiful creature of control promised you so much, it turned out to only get into your bloodstream and poison you. The zooids keep squeezing harder.

In truth, none of your worrying and stress will ever change an outcome. The painful reality is that you will never, ever be able to change another person. I hate this news; you probably do too.

It's also kind of the best realization ever.

It's the salve that lets you pull the stinging tentacles from your soul.

If you can't control or change the people around you, then what can you do? Turn to God, your Savior, who has the power to change people through His Word and Spirit. You can acknowledge that the true, deep joy you are looking for the whole time is peace.

You cannot heal your broken, terrified mind with your broken, terrified mind. But you can know, with crystal clarity, that God is working in slow, meaningful ways—or in bright flashes of dramatic awe—to bring all of His people to His plan of unity in eternity. Understand that the blue, iridescent tentacles of control are the worst illusion of all. Your mind will keep telling you to pick them up, but your soul knows the Spirit of God inspires a different way of living.

This is life at the pace of your Creator and Redeemer.

This is faith.

For Today

1. List all the parts of your life in which you have wrapped your tentacles of control around a person or a problem. How is this poisoning your faith? Talk (or write) about what the illusion of control does to the human spirit.

2. Read Romans 8:28. Write out what these words mean to you. What is God's purpose? How is His purpose often different than ours?

3. This week, write in your prayer journal about how God cares for you physically, emotionally, financially, and spiritually. Write prayers of thanksgiving for how your heavenly Father provides what you need to bring you closer to Him.

Challenge!

Write down one problem that you just can't stop worrying about. In a few sentences, tell God what about it makes you feel anxious. Then go for a walk. Pray, noticing how the Creator cares so well for nature and reflecting on how God has provided for you every day of your life. Rest in those promises and thank Him for His Spirit, who gives you faith. Later this evening, go back to the paper you wrote on and pray about the problem. Has God already given you peace about this? Continue to pray and trust that He will work all good things for you and for those who love Him in this season and situation.

Pray

Dear Father, take control of my life. I give You everything. You know the long view, and I trust You. In Your Son's name, I pray. Amen.

DAY 15

PENTECOST TOOLS

John answered them all, saying, "I baptize you with water, but He who is mightier than I is coming, the strap of whose sandals I am not worthy to untie. He will baptize you with the Holy Spirit and fire." (Luke 3:16)

Here's some of the best writing advice I ever heard: when writing a novel, your character should progress about ten degrees in every scene. After all, if the story is not going somewhere, your readers will put down the book to check Instagram.

At the halfway point of your month-long journey to live a more Spirit-centered life, your transformation might feel like a slow progression, just ten degrees every day. Maybe your life is a bit more Spirit-centered today than yesterday. Maybe some days—or even *several* days—you feel like you're stuck in the same old shame, paralysis, stubborn anger, and lack of faith. I get that. During some seasons, the old tools don't seem to be working for me anymore.

But what about the opposite times? What about the times when something changes, and your soul suddenly feels like it's on fire? What about those times when you have a new toolbox of ideas, relationships, and understanding of the Lord, and everything is a possibility?

These days feel like Pentecost all over again. Have you experienced days—or whole seasons—when it feels like the Holy Spirit rushes through you?

Perhaps this took place when you met someone you connected with in ministry. When this happened, you knew something else—this tide or fire or wind of the Holy Spirit—was leading you. You've forgiven or bonded with people in new ways, when there was only division and anger before. These moments hum with the knowledge that something holy is happening.

That's exactly how Luke describes the dramatic moments of Pentecost in Acts 2:1–4:

> When the day of Pentecost arrived, they were all together in one place. And suddenly there came from heaven a sound like a mighty rushing wind, and it filled the entire house where they were sitting. And divided tongues as of fire appeared to them and rested on each one of them. And they were all filled with the Holy Spirit and began to speak in other tongues as the Spirit gave them utterance.

In your toolbox are not only the fiery moments such as this but also the quiet moments that follow. The Holy Spirit works not only in His most dramatic ways but also in His most patient.

The Spirit works through the tools of slow, steady Bible study and through epiphanies of instant realization. He works through the tools of silent, contemplative prayer in the morning as well as through loud, raucous worship music in the afternoon. He works through the tools of Holy Communion as well as through your spiritual discussion with friends at a meal after church. The Spirit works through Baptism as well as through prayers at sunrise on the shore of a chilly lake.

Sometimes His work is in the exhilarating moments of Pentecost, and sometimes it's in the daily ministry of the new believers, as Luke describes in Acts 2:42–47:

> And they devoted themselves to the apostles' teaching and the fellowship, to the breaking of bread and the prayers. And awe came upon every soul, and many wonders and signs were being done through the apostles. And all who believed were together and had all things in common. And they were selling their possessions and belongings and distributing the proceeds to all, as any had need. And day by day, attending the temple together and breaking bread in their homes, they received their food with glad and generous hearts, praising God and having favor with all the people. And the Lord added to their number day by day those who were being saved.

What kind of transformation are you experiencing right now? What tools from your spiritual toolbox are you using? What is the Spirit doing in your life?

You might notice that when you're living deeply in the Holy Spirit, it often feels like you're out of step with the rest of the world—in a good way. This awkwardness is a solid indicator that the Holy Spirit is transforming your life. Your changed life is inspired by the deeper streams of bottomless faith, profound love, divine talents, and unfathomable peace.

But that experience does not always come through the same tools. Different seasons will mean that different tools might work for you right then. Don't give up if the old ones don't seem to be working. There are so many different ways to touch, feel, taste, and experience the power of the Spirit: a Pentecost outpouring; devoted teaching and learning; radical giving; regular worship; periods of very quiet stillness as you meditate on the words and promises of God.

Through it all, the Lord keeps working to bring His people closer to Him, through all the millions of tools that He gives us in this beautiful life.

For Today

1. Talk about the spiritual tools in your toolbox throughout your life. What has worship looked like throughout your life? What about Bible study? Tell the stories of what's worked in different seasons.

2. Read these verses from Luke: 4:42; 5:16; 6:12; 9:18, 28; 11:1; 22:39–41. In all of these verses, the apostle describes Jesus' habit of leaving the crowd to pray by Himself or with one or two disciples. Today, pray this same way. Be intentional about your surroundings. Make sure you have the space and quiet to sit and talk to God. Does this change your prayer time? How?

3. You have come this far in your spiritual transformation, thanks to both the trusty old and brand-new spiritual tools in your toolbox. Write a prayer to thank God for the ways He has used these tools to bless you over the years. Ask Him to give you fresh tools for times when you feel burnt out or anxious.

Challenge!

Find a new tool to add to your spiritual toolbox. Could you wake up five minutes earlier to begin the day with intentional prayer? What about calling a friend and committing to doing a Bible study together when you finish this one? (Even if she's far away, you could do it during a video call.) Or you could join a new service group at your church. Maybe it's a ministry that will send you on a mission trip, or maybe it's one that will have you filling busy bags for kids to use during the service. Whatever you are led to do, commit to it today.

Pray

> God of peace, fill my entire being with Your Holy Spirit so that I can live a life completely tethered to You. Help me to practice Your grace and peace every day. In Jesus' name, I pray. Amen.

Checking In on Your Progress

You Are Halfway There, and You Are Incredible—for Real

May the God of hope fill you with all joy and peace in believing, so that by the power of the Holy Spirit you may abound in hope. (Romans 15:13)

Hello!

Today is the halfway point! Woohoo! I'm so happy that you've made it this far. I am cheering you on as you do this brave work.

I'm also curious. How is all of this working for you? Are you keeping up with the reading? Is someone else checking in with you to hold you accountable? Where have you stumbled? What's kept you on track?

I'm praying for you—for all of you who are attempting this brave work right now. I'm asking God to help you see yourself a little differently than you did before. Most of all, I'm praying you are experiencing a faith transformation from the Holy Spirit. It's all over His Word—and that means it's a promise for you.

Drop me an email on my website (ChristinaHergenrader. com) and share a bit about how this work is going for you so far. I would love to hear your stories and what you're learning about and living through the Holy Spirit.

Here's what I'm praying for you:

May you feel bold in your skin, exactly as God created you. You're not an imposter at anything you are trying. You belong, dear one. Own that.

May you crave different, better experiences: less manufactured drama and way, way more vulnerable moments of real connection.

May you stop the constant diet of information that's making your head hurt. Soulful living means tuning into Scripture and worship to better understand God and who you are in Him.

May you detox from the false gods that made promises and never delivered. Peace is not here, dear one. Real joy will not be found in fake idols. Power is in God, peace comes from your true Savior, and your strength is from the Spirit.

May you believe the Holy Spirit calls, gathers, enlightens, and sanctifies the whole Christian church on earth and keeps it with Jesus Christ in the one true faith.

May you believe the Holy Spirit has called *you* by the Gospel, enlightened you with His gifts, sanctified and kept you in the true faith.

May you keep trying new things, creating, discovering, and inventing. More importantly, in a deeper way, may you see how the Spirit is always doing a new thing in you. Forgiveness, sanctification, new life: here is where the juiciness is. Live it out.

May the delicious fruits of the Spirit grow like crazy in you. Real change here, sister. Love, kindness, and peace are growing everywhere, and they are changing you, your family, your community, and the world. More of this, please. We all need it.

Onward, trooper! You're forming new habits that will last forever. Keep up the faithful work. God bless you as you finish the next two weeks of inspired living.

PRAISE

INSPIRED IN PRAISE: INTRODUCTION

As a deer pants for flowing streams, so pants my soul for You, O God. . . . Why are you cast down, O my soul, and why are you in turmoil within me? Hope in God; for I shall again praise Him, my salvation. (Psalm 42:1, 5)

Lately, I've been thinking a lot about the multi-billion-dollar movie industry. Isn't it interesting how much we love fantasy? Maybe it's a Disney fairy tale about a princess that gets the prince and, after that, the perfect ending. Perhaps it's one of the countless superhero movies that give unbelievable powers to the hero and villain. Regardless, we will pay anything to sit in a cool, dark room and see a better version of life that ends happily ever after.

Actually, movies are just the beginning of our love of fantasy. Aren't we all secretly holding out hope that something will change suddenly and dramatically in the hard slog of daily life?

In my own life, I can point to a shelf full of beauty creams that promise transformation while I sleep. I get dozens of emails every day from clothing stores that promise I'm one click away from the perfect outfit, at this unheard-of price. Most days, our front porch has a delivery box waiting to be opened. Inside will be the little toy or gadget or book or subscription that vowed to deliver a jolt of joy and efficiency to our lives.

Don't forget the constant news about politicians who have detailed plans finally to solve the problems of the human race and keep our country and families safe forever. Or the prescriptions or herbal supplements that promise to be the one thing your body has been missing your whole life.

Like you, our family lives in a museum of products that have not delivered what we had hoped they would. We have spent most of our time and money on the promise of something better. But truthfully, none of the things we have bought and invested in ever deliver the fantasy life playing out on our movie screen.

We worship food, clothes, spending power, influence, kids, friends, the feeling of belonging, an organized life, being informed, looking pretty, good schools, romantic love, a solid marriage, a beloved brand, the perfect home, an ideal weight, good health, family history, and being liked—to name a few.

All of these represent hope. No—it's more than "represent," and it's more than hope. Over and over, our human hearts worship these as saviors. We keep trading our adoration for a reality that will never, ever deliver.

That's why, when you think of it, it was a gutsy move for Jesus to come as an actual human being and live here on earth. John begins his Gospel with this surprise in 1:14: "And the Word became flesh and dwelt among us, and we have seen

His glory, glory as of the only Son from the Father, full of grace and truth."

This is it, folks: the actual Savior. He will be humble, live a perfect life, tell the truth we all need to hear, heal bodies and souls, and die for our sins. Flesh and blood, now appearing.

Then when that Savior leaves, He will give us the Holy Spirit, who will animate our souls and our lives with continuous spiritual nourishment. This very real divinity, Savior, hope, and eternal love is the one you and I need. God promises it, then delivers it through Jesus, then continues to sustain it through the Holy Spirit in every breath that each of His children takes.

That is something to worship. No, wait—that is the only thing to worship.

This week, that is what we will respond to: this real Savior, present through this Holy Spirit, in this precious moment of your life.

God is the one whom your soul desperately needs and loves. The Holy Spirit within you deeply desires for you to experience the extraordinary love of God and the hopeful expectation of eternal life with Him.

You might be complaining that you are still craving some potato chips. You might still believe that if your husband were more attentive, you would be happier, or if you just had an extra thousand dollars a month, your life could really be good. The human part of us loves this fantasy so much that we have trouble giving it up. Left on our own, we will always choose the illusion of human perfection instead of the reality of a divine Savior.

Meanwhile, your soul delights in the love of Jesus and who He is. The Holy Spirit is nudging you toward this experience, this relationship, these promises, this hope.

This worship.

Here's what I have found, and I pray you will too: real hope in a real Savior shows the truth about all the imitation saviors. When praise for my God is a regular part of my day, I am in the habit of looking to God to make me new, whole, loved, accepted, and transformed. I'm tuned into the humming frequency of the Spirit and the profound comfort of a real hope. I see that the gifts in my life are from God. I hear Jesus' words about not worrying. I sink into the Holy Spirit's authentic peace in my soul. All of that recalibrates my expectations of what a politician or a husband or online shopping can really give me.

Dear friends, don't waste your worship on promises that will never, ever deliver. Instead, rest in the promise of this very true and awesome God who does deliver everything you truly need. Sing the songs about who God is. Do your work in response to the opportunities He has given you. Love your neighbor because our Savior says to. Give cheerfully. Live a joyful life. Fast from meaningless spending or from social media. Make beautiful art. Tell people about Jesus. Play an instrument, sing, or dance. Sit in silence and acknowledge God's work in your soul.

This week, find out how worshiping your Savior changes you. Give your soul the nourishment it craves. Give all praise, love, and thanksgiving for your Creator, Redeemer, and Inspirer.

For Today

1. Talk (or write) about worship. Where do you find that you place a ridiculous amount of hope? How has reality shown you that this object of hope is not a savior?

2. Read Romans 1:21–23. How do you see this kind of worship in our culture? Talk about how we exchange the glory of the immortal God for those we create in our own image.

3. Pray this week, as you learn more about worship, to respond to the particular and wonderful life He has given you. Ask the Holy Spirit to stir in you to create faith and love for your Savior. Thank God for His gifts and love for you.

This Week

Get ready to look closely at fake gods in your life and dig into why you might have created them. Look ahead to the challenges for this week and structure your days around these. Finally, discover new ways to make worship a part of your daily habits.

Pray

Lord, Creator, heavenly Father, show me who You are and why I need Your love. Fill me with hope and gratitude. Cover me and my family with Your presence. Help me to respond to You in true praise. Amen.

DAY 17

WHEN YOU WORSHIP THE WORSHIP OF EVERYONE ELSE

And calling the crowd to Him with His disciples, He said to them, "If anyone would come after Me, let him deny himself and take up his cross and follow Me. For whoever would save his life will lose it, but whoever loses his life for My sake and the gospel's will save it. For what does it profit a man to gain the whole world and forfeit his soul? For what can a man give in return for his soul?" (Mark 8:34-37)

Part of learning how to live a more inspired life is taking a close look at what you worship. Our human hearts are always looking for idols. Our minds are constantly searching for something to make us feel safe, numb, loved, or alive. These appear in the strangest packaging.

One of the biggest and shiniest idols in most of our lives is wanting to be liked. To accomplish that, you might have become everyone's "yes girl." You fill in and sign up and carry other people's workloads, just so you can feel needed. You say yes to whatever someone asks, as long as it means you can feel that wonderful, toxic exhilaration of being needed.

If you've been at this for a while, you know how it ends. Praise and approval act like MSG. The more you taste them, the hungrier you are.

Maybe it isn't praise or love you worship, but something else. Many moms worship their children, and they try to hold on to their affection forever. So many of us worship the image of control in the form of huge homes, beautiful lawns, swoon-worthy closets, and sparkling-clean kitchens. Almost everyone I know pins big dreams on getting healthier, more efficient, a little more financially secure.

If you're like me, you worship authority. Maybe you learned at a really young age that the decision-maker in the room was the person to impress. You've been a team player for years, with the hope that this approval gives you profound security.

The problem is that all of these idols are temporary and ridiculously flimsy idols. When the people, money, or power structure you've worshiped collapse, it causes all kinds of other problems. You might find that you're resentful that you gave so much to a boss who turned out to be flawed. Or maybe, when a few people let you down, you become bitter and cynical toward all people.

This is all crazy, of course. Such flawed institutions can't handle that kind of pressure; they were never meant to. Yet so many of us keep stubbing our toes on these supports. We keep handing praise to something that can't handle it.

Part of learning to live more soulfully gets right to that question: what false idol do you worship, and why? Sit with that question for a minute. What people or systems or things do you believe in so strongly that you hand your trust, love, and adoration to them again and again?

More importantly, what soul sickness are you trying to heal? What low-grade fever of anxiety do you need to allay? Are you allergic to the sting of rejection? Are you struggling with the malaise of being unlovable? Are you fatigued with fear?

Here is a truth we all have to face: more work, more responsibility, more stuff, and more dependents will not heal any of these maladies. In fact, on the other side is just more work, more responsibility, more stuff, and more dependents. So if you're doing something in an attempt to feel more loved, you will not find love here.

You are a soul, not a role. So much of the work and clutter you pile into your life is just taking up space for the wrong reason. To prune that from your life, start with this question: am I holding on to this to feel safe? Because stuff and responsibility can never provide the security you already have from your Savior.

They were never meant to.

In the name of real worship, be done with the false idols. Donate the clutter, quit the hustle, and keep your loved ones off a pedestal. True worship begins with what the Holy Spirit is doing in your spirit: giving you faith in God.

Devote yourself to that, and discover the deep, authentic love you've been looking for all along.

For Today

1. What idols have you created in your life? Talk (or write) about your relationship with your kids or family—do you find yourself searching for more love than they can provide? What about money and things? How about your roles as friend and employee? Are you hoping for soul-deep security from these things?

2. Read Galatians 4:1–7. What does it mean to be adopted by God instead of living as a slave? Look at verses 6–7. Talk (or write) about the security and love in this description of God. What does this mean specifically to you right now?

3. Pray for God to help you prune your life from false idols. List three false gods you worship right now. They might include money, power, friends, success, or security. Ask God to reveal these as things to which you have become a slave. Pray that He will show you that you are more and more entrenched in the cycle of worshiping the wrong things. Lay those idols down at God's altar, and ask the Holy Spirit to create a clean heart and renew a right spirit within you.

Challenge!

Prune a false idol from your life today by ridding yourself of a false savior. Ask God for courage and wisdom as you choose what to quit so that you can create more space in your life to worship the true Savior. Unsubscribe from all the emails that announce products and sales that promise to give you happiness but end up just delivering more clutter. Quit a volunteer role that is taking time away from your chance to be in a Bible study. Look at other roles in your life—mother or employee or wife—and ask yourself if you're serving in those roles as a response to Christ's love for you or as a way to find security. Write about what you discover and what you need to do to change your habits.

Pray

Dear Jesus, give me faith, perspective, and courage to worship only You. Help me to see the false idols in my life and prune those from my day. Give me the desire to look to You to be loved and secure. Amen.

DAY 18

LIMITATIONS AND INVITATIONS

For if you live according to the flesh you will die, but if by the Spirit you put to death the deeds of the body, you will live. For all who are led by the Spirit of God are sons of God. (Romans 8:13-14)

A few months ago, I joined a group of creative people who gathered to talk about ways we feel stuck. A pastor was with us too. He's the kind of person who is especially good at asking hard questions and offering unconventional solutions. For thirty minutes, each of us sat in front of the group, with the pastor in the front of the room, to brainstorm ways to improve ministry. The other writers, artists, and speakers listened and helped us imagine new solutions to ministry problems.

I was there because I had been feeling stuck in my ministry to teens. As both a teacher and writer for high school students, I could see how their dependence on technology was damaging them. More and more, they were disconnected from actual conversations and relationships. Parents were wringing their hands about the anxiety and depression that swallowed up their teens. I desperately wanted to write a book or give a talk that would teach parents that the first step of connecting with their sons and daughters was to make them put down their devices. But how could I drive home this message?

As I explained this to the pastor and circle of fellow creatives, the room was quiet. Because, really, no one knew. Also, to a certain extent, this was a problem we were all facing in our ministry. How can we get our modern generation to trade the comfort of a digital world for the vulnerability of in-person connections?

The pastor listened and then asked, "Do you think a book is really the best way to teach this? What if, instead, you *showed* them real connection? What if you lived out exactly what you want them to know? What if you invited them to your house, gathered around your table, ate good food, and talked?"

As soon as I heard this wise pastor's suggestions, I knew this was the right path. Everyone else in that room knew it too. Of course. Silence settled over all of us as we realized that anxious teens and parents didn't need another lecture, another book, another prescription for how to live. They needed an example, a model of what connecting looked like. They needed to feel the blessings of true relationships that come when you sit face-to-face, talk about your day, laugh at silly stories, and share about what's challenging right now.

I left that meeting filled with ideas, excitement, and plans. I would just go home and invite over a bunch of teens and their parents. I would feed them, and they would soften, talk, and connect, and they would love it. I would single-handedly save the next generation! No problem!

It didn't happen that way. Instead, I came home to the reality of our crazy busy lives—and my own anxiety about the extreme awkwardness of the idea. The more I thought about it, the crazier it sounded. What was I going to say in the text to invite people over? Something like, "Hey! Just trying to change the next generation with some face-to-face connection. Come over on Friday night. I know you probably have at least twelve other places to be, but I'll make mediocre spaghetti, and we can all chat." Nope. Embarrassing. Terrible idea.

For the next few months, every time I heard about teen suicide or looked at the face of another highly distracted teen, I thought about that plan. Then I thought about all the problems with this idea: no one would come because no one had time, feeding a dozen or so people would be fairly expensive, and our house was not really company-ready. Ever.

Except mixed in with my fear and excuses was also the advice someone had given at that artists' roundtable: look for the invitation in the limitations. In other words, every idea has roadblocks, but look at them as opportunities to get creative. Problems are places to grow. There is always—always—something that every difficulty can teach you.

At the same time, the Holy Spirit kept nudging me about the idea. First, I had a few conversations with dear friends about feeling disconnected. These friends said the same thing I had said to that group many months before: "People are feeling a need to do real life with real people." That's interesting. Same words.

Also, our kids kept talking about how they wanted to have friends over. They didn't talk about wanting to go to other houses. They asked to invite friends to our house.

Okay. Not that subtle, so I doubled down on my excuse about not having time. I even went to my husband for backup.

"We are so busy! Can you imagine us having a whole bunch of people over every Sunday night?"

But he didn't answer with the expected, "Our weekends are too full." Instead, he hedged. "I don't know. I think we could pull it off. Let's just make the food and see if anyone will come. Maybe, since everyone is busy, we can use it as an excuse to keep the whole thing really simple."

Limitations. Invitations.

Then, as if I needed more reasons to get over my fear and do this, our sixteen-year-old daughter came to me and said she wanted deeper friendships. It had been hard to move to a new school, and she recognized that it was time to get closer with the people she had met. She rattled off a list of names of people we should have over.

Sure enough, at the next football game, I ran into a few of those very people. When they said the same old, "We should get together!" I followed it with, "Yes. Sunday night at 6 p.m. Can you be there?"

To our astonishment, they all came. Four other families and their twelve collective teenagers. And it was a tiny bit awkward at first. We served chili and cinnamon rolls. We pulled out some games and the bead kit that our girls liked to use when they were hanging out and chatting. The adults gathered in the dining room and laughed and talked. The kids sat in a circle and grabbed handfuls of beads and made little bracelets.

Everyone had a good time—like, a really good time. When we walked them out, a mom I didn't know very well casually said how long they had been wanting to do this.

Just like that, our Sunday-night dinners had begun. We've had people over every week for months now. Every time, there's a limitation. (To be honest, it's usually my anxiety about our messy house or my lackluster kitchen skills.) But from our limitations, we are learning much-needed lessons.

We have learned to relax about the embarrassment that our house looks very lived-in. Really, we should have accepted this a long time ago. Why feel ashamed, when it just makes others feel more at home to see that our couch is also stained? And to see that we also aren't great about remembering to wipe out the microwave?

We have also learned to stop being so serious about meals with other people. Because, really, gathering people around the table is the most ancient of practices. No one is there for the food. They are there to connect.

Also, strange, spiritual things seemed to happen with our Sunday-night dinners, like loaves-and-fishes kinds of moments. The length of our Sundays felt exponential. It used to seem like the hours after church slid right into prepping for the next week. Once we started inviting people over for these dinners, we suddenly seemed to have all this time. Also, there is always (always!) just the right food and people. We learned that even tacos taste better when you're laughing about the ridiculousness of parenthood with a bunch of other people who are in the same season as you.

We've learned so much from these Sunday-night dinners. Mostly that these in-person times with our friends and family that have allowed those relationships to deepen are just like our in-person times with God. He deepens our relationship with Him. Think about it: God was in-person with humanity when He breathed life into Adam. The Bible is full of stories about real life with real people. The most amazing are ones about Jesus. God was literally in-person when Jesus was born. And God literally touched people to heal them and open their eyes to Him. He is still in-person with us when we read His Word, when we go to church, and when we receive His Holy Supper. These are links to Him, ways He cares for us.

What about you? What limitations are you facing right now? What are you afraid to try? What feels awkward and too personal?

And where is the invitation in this idea? Is there something God is urging you to do that just doesn't seem logical? Do the problems with the plan outweigh the idea? What could you learn from those problems—a new way to do it? Perhaps it's a new understanding of how this has already been done. Most important, when God calls you, He also equips you.

For Today

1. Think of a recent idea you've had. Write about it or talk about it here. What are the limitations? What invitations for more curiosity, questioning, or courageous faith are here as well?

2. Read Hebrews 13:20–21. What miracle does God work in us? How is the description in this verse significant?

3. Ask God for something you need right now to accomplish His will. Ask Him for strength, hope, vision, and determination to do the plans that He has for you. Keep a journal about how God blesses you and equips you to accomplish His will.

Challenge!

God is working in you about an idea, a relationship, a problem, or a fear you have right now. Write, draw, or say what's been on your heart lately. Next, write one limitation that scares you about this. Finally, write what invitation God might have for you here. Draw a box around that invitation. This invitation is your assignment for today. Pray about it, and then make the hard call, extend the offer to connect with a friend, take the next step that is written in that box. Ask someone you know well to hold you accountable to trust that the Holy Spirit can turn this limitation into an invitation.

Pray

Lord, Creator, heavenly Father, change my perspective to Your perspective, dear God. Fill me with Your plans and faith from the Holy Spirit. Amen.

COMPLETELY AND TOTALLY IN AWE

In that same hour He rejoiced in the Holy Spirit and said, "I thank You, Father, Lord of heaven and earth, that You have hidden these things from the wise and understanding and revealed them to little children; yes, Father, for such was Your gracious will." (Luke 10:21)

We've had a weird weather week here in Houston. In twenty-four hours, Tropical Storm Beta dumped fifteen inches of rain on our community. School was canceled, roads flooded, those who live near the coast lost their homes, and the population of Houston (millions of people) was captivated by the hourly updates of when this storm would stop drenching us with its torrential rains.

Maybe in your part of the world, it's been blizzards, terrible wildfires, earthquakes, tornadoes, or even a volcano. You know the drill—these catastrophic acts of nature tap into our deepest feelings of being powerless. You tune into the news or social media or your favorite meteorologist's Twitter page to learn what's happening and how to protect yourself and your people.

Our family tuned in to the wise words of our favorite meteorologist, Eric Berger. When there is a storm in the Gulf of Mexico, millions of people wait for his forecast to decide what to do. Not only is he a really good scientist who understands complex weather patterns, but he also delivers his forecasts with a profound understanding of how each weather system will affect our community.

After the tropical storm dumped all its precipitation on us, Texans opened their front doors to discover that the storm had left behind glorious, cool weather. After many months of hot, humid air that felt like we were trapped in a dryer, the moisture and heat cleared out of the atmosphere and left the kind of crisp, cool weather that makes people want to buy pumpkin-flavored drinks and bake banana bread.

Since our region was so ready to change out of shorts and tank tops, everyone gave the first day of fall-like weather a giant hug. Instead of grilling steaks, the aroma we had smelled for months, our neighbor burned a small pile of leaves. Our kids insisted on hot chocolate for breakfast. I put on my best over-sized sweatshirt and made plans to cheer on our high school football team at the first game of the season. Just like that, it was magically fall. And it was glorious.

As we visited a farmer's market that afternoon and picked out pumpkins, I wondered how our beloved meteorologist welcomed this splendid, sudden change of season. He surely knew it was coming. The science of dry air and wind shear—or whatever the right term is; clearly, I have no real idea—meant he could predict exactly how this wonderful day would feel.

Scientifically, he understood it on so many levels. Did that also mean he would not be in awe of the beautiful weather?

Would understanding this as a meteorologist taint the wonder of how superbly good it felt to finally have a chill in the air?

This challenge affects all of us. We have so much trouble turning off the constant information-analyzing machine of our brains to really appreciate anything.

Try playing your absolute favorite song for someone. You know the one—the beautiful music that sweeps you away with the power of the melody and gorgeous harmonies and exquisite lyrics?

Have you ever put that music on and waited for the other person to listen with awe at the power of the art? And then, instead, have they immediately started *talking* about it? Analyzing it? Telling you what they think about it rather than just experiencing it? You want to tell them to stop—sit in wonder of this with me, feel this, soak it up. We'll examine it later; for now, let's live in the beauty of the moment together.

Ah, friends, worship can feel like this, can't it? Our minds come to church with a meteorologist's understanding of what should scientifically be happening. We analyze how Communion is distributed or think how we would have chosen a different hymn or consider the way that the pastor phrased a specific theological point.

Instead of tasting this holy moment, we are scrutinizing the recipe. Our souls are like thirsty deer, panting for the water of God's Word and gifts of the Sacraments. But our minds keep ruining the moment with loud speeches about how this could be better—if only someone would tell the pastor to keep the sermon shorter.

Worship is a sacred event, reverberating outside of space and time. This nourishment is what your soul needs right now—the wonder of God's promises and the infinite love of

His Son, Jesus. Sit there with your eyes closed and turn off your analyzing mind. Refuse to criticize, analyze, and judge. For this moment, just be.

You came here for this shiver of the Holy Spirit down your spine and through the pit of your soul. You came to be in awe of our Creator and what He is making new in your life right now.

You came to be amazed.

For Today

1. Talk about a part of your life in which you struggle to experience rather than analyze. What causes this struggle for you? Are you anxious for things to happen according to the rules? Do you desire to have the right answer? Do you feel a need for the correct form and function?

2. Which part of the worship service captures your mind the most? Is it the music, the Sacrament of Communion, the beauty of the words of the Absolution, the promise in the Scriptures, or hearing the Gospel proclaimed? Write about that here.

3. Whenever you feel the temptation to move into analytical mode, take five very slow, deep breaths and hear what God is saying to you.

Challenge!

When you receive Holy Communion, you receive Jesus' true body and blood, and with Your Savior, you receive the Holy Spirit. Today, describe what that experience has meant for you over your lifetime. Write a journal entry about the Lord's Supper throughout your life—when you first received Communion, what happens in the Eucharist, and what hope you have for your faith in the Sacrament.

Pray

Heavenly Father, help me to live in awe and wonder of You. Nourish my soul with Your words, and help me to worship You. Amen.

DAY 20

Hold the World Loosely

If then you have been raised with Christ, seek the things that are above, where Christ is, seated at the right hand of God. Set your minds on things that are above, not on things that are on earth. For you have died, and your life is hidden with Christ in God. When Christ who is your life appears, then you also will appear with Him in glory. (Colossians 3:1–4)

Right now, several interesting (and stressful) new developments are happening in our family. First, our oldest daughter, Catie, is learning to drive. Second, our oldest son, Sam, is playing select baseball for the first time. Honorable mention (because motherhood is never dull) goes to our daughter, Elisabeth, who is determined to keep every one of her grades above 95 percent. Oh, and also to our youngest son, Nate, who is learning to play the clarinet.

You might think this sounds like a loud, stressful, angsty season in the Hergenrader house—and you would certainly be right. Every one of these things is a process, and in every process, you can find failure at every turn. Two steps forward and three steps back on all of it.

My son needs to learn to settle into his personal swing just right so he can stop striking out. Our new driver needs to figure out how to brake with the right force not only so that she doesn't hit the car in front of her but also so that she doesn't give her passengers whiplash. Our younger daughter is trying to learn to read the mind of her seventh-grade science teacher so she can predict what to study for his killer tests. And, oh, the clarinet. Our youngest is trying and trying to learn to hold his lips just right to get the clarinet to hum with music instead of *squeeeeaaaaak*.

We're learning in this season of new skills that becoming good at something is counterintuitive. With all of these activities—batting, driving, studying, and playing a musical instrument—our instinct is to hold it all so tight. Work harder. Double down on your focus. Beat yourself up over any mistake. Clench your jaw and ramrod yourself into the process to grab the skills you need.

But that won't work at all.

I'm writing this just after coming home from a baseball tournament, where my son approached the plate with a spine stiffer than the bat and hands shaking from white-knuckling it. In the parking lot, our new driver was so focused on not hitting one car that she didn't see another coming toward her.

The same goes for our child scholar and budding clarinetist. Over and over, we tell them that the key to scoring well on a test and making beautiful music is *relaxing*. The ironclad grip doesn't work because it doesn't allow for the much-needed mistakes. To all of our kids right now, we keep saying, "Hold all of this loosely." Yes, if you ease up on the bat, you might strike out, but you also settle into your swing. When you relax your shoulders and take deep breaths, you're a less anxious (and thus better) driver. To play an instrument, you really do need to sense out the notes and how they feel in your mouth. You just can't do that when you're clenching your muscles.

Dear friends, this lesson applies to all of life. What are you holding too tightly right now? Maybe it's the marriage you need to succeed, and you're squeezing it so tight there's no life left in it. Or maybe it's the job, the finances, the title, the friend group, or the persona that you are white-knuckling for it to look exactly perfect. Anything less scares you to death. Because of that, no one around you can breathe or see straight for fear of doing something wrong.

This tight grip is the opposite of living an inspired life. This toxic, saccharine perfectionism is living with your ego in control. But can you see that this was never the life God wanted you to lead?

Really, this message is all throughout Scripture—especially in Colossians 3:1–4: "Seek the things that are from above, where Christ is seated on the right hand of God" (v. 1). Focus less on the temporary, false promises of earth. Instead, soak up the eternal, love-filled grace of your Savior.

Your Father has this whole other plan for you, in which you abide in His grace (Colossians 3:4). In that life, you get to be creative and try new things to see if He blesses it.

You don't have to work to get approval from others. You don't need to wedge yourself into where you don't belong because you wholly belong to Him. This approach is incredibly different from looking over your life and demanding constant perfection and compliance from everyone around you. In fact, it's completely and totally opposite.

When we study Scripture, we see that the Holy Spirit works in our soul in a way that doesn't make sense. It's more miraculous, surprising, and joy-filled than the plans you were writing in your rigid, demanding scrawl.

Ease up on the bat. Relax your hands on the wheel. Take a deep breath and pray for God to help you learn what you need to know. Close your eyes and play the most beautiful music of God's grace in your life.

For Today

1. So much more is available to you than a small life built out of high expectations and rigid perfectionism. In what ways do you find you're pinning yourself into a very small, tightly controlled space where only success and anxiety are allowed?

2. Read 2 Corinthians 12:9. What weakness is part of your process? How do you need God's grace? How can you show this grace to yourself?

3. Ask God to bless you with the very gifts you need right now to equip you for the life He has given you. Pray for Him to give you every fruit of the Spirit (love, joy, peace, patience, kindness, goodness, faithfulness, gentleness, and self-control).

Challenge!

Write a letter to yourself about something you're holding too tightly. Maybe it's a relationship; often it's the relationship with your spouse, your kids, or your parents. Remind yourself of God's grace in 2 Corinthians 12:9. What are you afraid will happen if you ease up on this? Write that in the letter! Then remind yourself of God's promise that He will still work—that His best work comes—in our shortcomings. End by writing out the words to the Bible verse.

Pray

Dear Jesus, thank You for living a perfect life so I don't have to. Help me to trust the process of confession, repentance, and forgiveness, and to rest in Your promise of constant love. I love You. Amen.

DAY 21

FAIL BETTER

Not only that, but we rejoice in our sufferings, knowing that suffering produces endurance, and endurance produces character, and character produces hope, and hope does not put us to shame, because God's love has been poured into our hearts through the Holy Spirit who has been given to us. (Romans 5:3-5)

My friends and I were talking the other day about what it means to be a younger sister. We decided that growing up in our families, it seemed easier to be the youngest because there are lower expectations of us. Everyone was paying attention to what the oldest child was doing because it was the first time anyone in the family had ever seen a child in their family walk, talk, play soccer, go on a date, or get married. In some families, there's so much angst, perfection, and responsibility tied up in being the oldest child.

My husband, Mike, is a quintessential oldest child—he follows the rules, feels responsible to fill out all the forms and get the payment in on time, and wants to make sure it's all done right. I love him for this, and it's absolutely one of the reasons our life together clicks so well.

What I bring to our marriage is the other perspective—that it's okay if we don't make the recipe exactly, that it's more exciting to meander through the back roads than follow the map, and wouldn't it be fun if we had a theme dinner where everyone dressed as *Star Wars* characters?

This creativity—and not taking life too seriously—is a gift of being the youngest child: your parents were just not paying that much attention to you. The more influential person in your childhood may have been an older sibling, and this person was not afraid to tell you when you were doing something stupid or flat-out reject you and tell you that you were too young, dumb, or annoying to play the game your cool older sibling was creating.

Can you see the gift this was for that youngest child? This kind of social failure opened the rest of her life to very low expectations.

As a result, when we youngest kids create something, try a new job, or move to a new place, we're okay with the possibility that it won't go well. Long ago, in our most formative years, we developed a strong ability to keep trying! Youngest children just don't get too hung up on success.

This gift of rejection and social failure gave me the freedom to be creative. For anyone who tries to make something new, you know that most of the process is lots of failure. In fact, failure is probably the most important part of the activity.

You mess up, try another way, edit this, and delete that. You flop at the original plan, but in the process, you find a little gem that had been waiting for you to discover it. Through it, you find the cracks that let the light in and blow open all kinds of new possibilities.

Being okay with rejection allows for much more freedom. When you're super okay with crashing and burning, you stop putting your identity in the success. Instead, you get really curious about what happens next. This freedom to explore is the backstory of every success, every invention, every restored relationship, every road trip, every plan.

This process is happening in your soul all the time, thanks to the work of the Holy Spirit. You fail; the Spirit reconstructs your life. You sin; the Spirit offers forgiveness and a clean heart. You fall apart; the Spirit rebuilds you.

Actually, this reconstruction is also the story of just about everyone in the Bible. They find themselves on the totally wrong path—one that pulled them from God. Then God convicts them, forgives them, and gives them a new plan and a new heart.

It's hard to try, fail, try again, pivot, fail again, learn new lessons, and try again. It can be excruciating. Your flesh doesn't want to admit it doesn't have everything figured out yet.

We're far from perfect, and we need God's love-edits in our lives. But soulful living means hearing His voice and changing your life better to fit the plan He has for you.

Perhaps the hardest part of getting older (and wiser) is not becoming cynical or stuck. Be more curious than scared. Why not keep discovering, making new things, and finding better ways? Your security is in God. Be pliable to the Holy Spirit forming you.

Let's stay this way. Forget your old brain that would tell you failure looks bad and that if it doesn't work the first time, it's not worth doing. Instead, engage in the process, stay flexible, and listen to your Lord.

Fail. Fail again. Fail better. Allow God to work through this practice. Trust the Holy Spirit. This next chapter is going to be amazing.

For Today

1. Tell the story of a recent time you've had to pivot. What failed? How did you initially react? What better lesson or new thing came from the experience?

2. Consider the life of Joseph in the Book of Genesis. Think of how many times it seemed like he failed and had to change his plan. What do you notice about how he doesn't get stuck? Write about or discuss with the group at least three times that Joseph could have reacted to the events of his life by being cynical and stuck. What did he do instead? How did listening to God and recognizing God's work in his life change Joseph? How did he serve as a witness to his friends, family, community, and us?

3. Pray for God to keep your will pliable and your security firmly in Him. Ask your heavenly Father to keep you flexible to His plans for your life. Ask the Holy Spirit to show the fruit of the Spirit in your life and in your relationships.

Challenge!

Today, you're going to try something new. Choose something you've been wanting to do that has a high probability of rejection and that you will most likely fail at—and then do it anyway. Call someone you haven't talked to in years and who you maybe even get the feeling doesn't like you. Tell someone you admire exactly how you feel, even if it's someone you barely know, such as the barista who makes your coffee. Let yourself be vulnerable in the process, trusting that no matter what happens, you will learn something new. Say the honest truth with no fear of rejection. You are always secure in God's love for you. This fun experiment explores living wholly in that Spirit and opening yourself up to the process of deeper flexibility.

Pray

Dear Jesus, thank You for Your sacrifice so I can be forgiven over and over. Keep me flexible and allow me to fail, completely secure that Your grace never fails. As always, keep me close to You. Amen.

DAY 22

WHAT ARE YOU PRACTICING?

For this reason I remind you to fan into flame the gift of God, which is in you through the laying on of my hands, for God gave us a spirit not of fear but of power and love and self-control. (2 Timothy 1:6–7)

One of our kids is naturally very creative. He is fidgety with curiosity. He is constantly exploring, tinkering, asking questions, and making art, music, and inventions.

I've noticed something interesting about his process, though. When his experiments don't turn out as he expects, or when he starts to lose interest, he abandons the creativity and looks for something to consume. Usually, he scrolls through videos to watch other people create. Or he can get lost for hours on shopping websites, looking at products and reading reviews. Or he heads to the pantry for a Twizzler.

He does this because it's what we all do. Not only in the Hergenrader family—although we certainly do that—but also all of humankind, forever and ever. We have the urge to create, but we can't stand the fear and failure that's tied up in the process.

It happens millions of times a day, over the whole world. So many people with so many ideas, dreams, thoughts, and plans to make new things. But at some point in the process of trying to create something, the plan doesn't work out like the vision. The painting looks a little silly. The bookshelf is crooked. The stitches are wonky. The poem is way too sappy. The photograph is too cheesy. The rabbits dug up the garden. The new turquoise kitchen looks like a fast-food restaurant.

The effort to try to make something and then failing strikes a paralyzing fear deep in the gut of the artist. Every time. The cocktail of shame and terror is always poisonous. We have all tasted that and know how it kills curiosity, creativity, and faith.

Over and over, if you are like me, you settle for the lamest substitute: you consume instead of create. This turns out to be just about the safest interaction with your environment. You practice scrolling, eating, binge-watching, or shopping.

Consuming usually does a pretty good job of numbing your desire to create. Mindless consumption helps erase failure, fear, and humiliation. Well, it kind of does.

Now that you're binging home improvement shows, it's easier to forget about that letter you've been meaning to write—the one to your oldest friend, who is a fresh widow and in a world of hurt. You had planned to tell her all about your favorite memory with her dearly departed husband. You could feel how she would love to hear the story about the boat and how hard you all laughed that day out on the water. But what if you butcher the story? What if you get it wrong? Or, worse, what if you somehow insult her? What if you remind her of him, and it makes her feel worse?

So it's better to just scroll your social media accounts and like the dumb memes that everyone is posting about a television show that you kind of hate. It's safer this way. Isn't life supposed to be about always staying safe and in control and never looking silly? (If it is, you are totally winning.)

But there's still that humming curiosity, buzzing through your soul. What do you do with that? Well, you can always satisfy that nagging urge to make something by strolling through your favorite department store and seeing what new candles they have. That kind of satisfies the itch. You can sedate in another way the part of you that wants to go into the kitchen with sharp knives, measuring cups, and your favorite recipes. You could just pull out your secret stash of peanut-butter-cup ice cream and eat a pint over the sink. That's practically the same thing as cooking a delicious new recipe, right?

Of course, it's totally not the same thing. Creating is a work of possibility, union, kindness, faith, wonder, thrill, and beauty. It's a response to the individuality God designed you to have. It's trust that He can make something that wasn't there before. It's the vulnerability to connect with someone who needs it. It's taking a risk in the best way: a tiny glimpse of what God did in making the universe and what the Holy Spirit does in your soul to make faith. Nothing—then something. Think of the hymns, poems, paintings, books, plays, musicals, buildings, and expressions of love and joy that have come from creating. Creativity is where we can see God giving and sharing with His people.

Consuming, on the other hand, is taking and not giving. It is fear, shame, judgment, paralysis, gluttony, and repression. It's more clutter, calories, burdens, and chaos that you don't need. It's weak, guilt-inducing, and greedy. So much of our current culture is built on consuming. It's too much, too much, too much. We keep doing it because it's easier—until it's not.

I'm learning this too. Each of us is practicing some habit in our one, beautiful life. We are practicing either creativity or consumption. We are practicing either faith or fear. Every minute of every day is a little choice. In the end, these choices add up to what we have created—or consumed.

As God's favorite creation, we have a divine curiosity about how to create a more beautiful, efficient, extraordinary life. We humans have used the ingenuity and creativity God gives us to make this world more beautiful, efficient, and understandable. We use creativity to praise Him and give Him credit for all we have, do, and are.

It comes down to what you are practicing. Trust the better choice. Open your heart to the explosions of beauty and joy that live in your creativity.

Live with vulnerability—and create.

For Today

1. What habits are you practicing right now? When you have the urge to create something, do you find that you get frustrated? Do you often end up consuming instead? What could you do to change this habit?

2. Look at Jesus' message in Matthew 6:19–20. What is His message about the things that really last? Think about your life right now. What have you seen "moth and rust destroy" (v. 19)?

3. Pray for the Holy Spirit to give you confidence to make and create blessings for other people. Ask for the curiosity to lead you into new ways to express your faith. Read Hebrews 11:1–3 and pray these words: "Lord, give me faith to be sure of what I cannot see. Bless me with the vision to see things that are not visible. Bless my work so that it may be a blessing to many and share Your love. Amen."

Challenge!

Inject one little bit of creativity into your daily habits. Starting today, write a short text to someone who has been a blessing in your life. Your words can be as simple or as elaborate as you want. As the days go on, also draw a little picture about what they have meant to you, and text that to the person. On days you have time, practice generosity and bake cookies for the person and deliver or mail them with a hand-decorated note.

Pray

Lord, by Your grace, I reject the fear that would paralyze my faith and my service. Instead, fill me with Your Spirit. May the Holy Spirit animate my life with generosity, confidence, and curiosity. In Jesus' name, I pray. Amen.

REFLECTION

Inspired in Reflection: Introduction

What good is it, my brothers, if someone says he has faith but does not have works? Can that faith save him? If a brother or sister is poorly clothed and lacking in daily food, and one of you says to them, "Go in peace, be warmed and filled," without giving them the things needed for the body, what good is that? So also faith by itself, if it does not have works, is dead.

But someone will say, "You have faith and I have works." Show me your faith apart from your works, and I will show you my faith by my works. You believe that God is one; you do well. Even the demons believe—and shudder! Do you want to be shown, you foolish person, that faith apart from works is useless? Was not Abraham our father justified by works when he offered up his son Isaac on the altar? You see that faith was active along *with his works, and faith was completed by his works; and the Scripture was fulfilled that says, "Abraham believed God, and it was counted to him as righteousness"—and he was called a friend of God. You see that a person is justified by works and not by faith alone. And in the same way was not also Rahab the prostitute justified by works when she received the messengers and sent them out by another way? For as the body apart from the spirit is dead, so also faith apart from works is dead. (James 2:14-26)*

I have written books and had the chance to speak about how to show grace. Grace in our families, grace to our literal next-door neighbors, grace in our church, and grace in our communities.

I don't have to tell you that grace is missing from much of what's unfolding in each and every one of our stories. I'm not talking about tolerance here; I'm talking about deep, selfless, joyfully given grace—the kind that Jesus describes, God shows, and the Holy Spirit enables.

However, there was a time when I was a little cynical about grace. I felt like I was talking about grace all the time, and studying grace was actually my job. I kept teaching the same lessons about grace: show up, have low expectations of other people, and forgive as Jesus did. I talked about grace until I had no more words left—and it was not enough.

The best example I can give for describing grace is this: all of these people are in the deep end of the swimming pool, floundering and gasping for help, and our church (including me!) keeps yelling to them, "What you need right now is a big, deep breath of oxygen!" and "Hey! Why don't you try to swim?" or "I suggest that you get out of the pool now!" or my favorite, "Let me analyze why you might be struggling here." Or the response most of the world believes Christians give: "If you're drowning, it's probably your own fault."

Super helpful for those weak from struggling and just about to go under, right?

What good are those instructions shouted from the side-lines? How helpful are diagrams of the proper breaststroke when the person's lungs are filling with water?

There has to be something else.

And there is. There is an animating force that drives you and me to trust God, to risk our own safety to get in the water and to demonstrate the strokes to show people the way to the life raft that's *right there.*

The Holy Spirit is this animating force that inspires spiritual living. This is Jesus revealing the Holy Spirit to His disciples in John 14:17 and saying to them, "You know Him, for He dwells with you and will be in you." Jesus taught His followers to show real grace by loving and forgiving others. Jesus sends us out in His name, equipped with the wind and fire of the Holy Spirit.

We live this out when we do what James says in chapter 2 of his epistle. An inspired life is not only about analyzing God's Word, but it is also about getting food to hungry people, show-ing up in the middle of our family's messy dramas, praying with the hurting, and caring for the most vulnerable. Flesh and blood—fully present. Just like Jesus.

The Holy Spirit in action is the breath and life that our world desperately needs. He brings radical forgiveness for you and those who have hurt you. This change is just not something we can conjure up on our own. This is inspiration, sister. Through Him, we can live differently than the rest of the world does.

That's what we are all looking for—inspiration to be something different, something holy, something not of this world.

Through inspiration, we reflect the messages we see in God's Word. Hearing the Word ignites faith, followed by holy comprehension, then spiritual transformation, and ultimately illumination that allows us to reflect God's love to the world through our actions.

This week, you will have the chance to experience this spiritual conversion from knowledge to action. Through creating and writing, you will live out life ignited by the Holy Spirit.

Ah, this inspiration is the breath you have needed. When your soul is fortified with this love, showing grace is the organic response. It's not created in your head; God creates it, and it's lived through your soul, your heart, your mind, and your body.

This grace and love are what we will talk about understanding, digesting, transforming, and sharing with the world, through action.

For Today

1. Talk (or write) about what reflection looks like in your life. How are you living out the Gospel? What strengthening or encouragement do you need here? What would transformation look like for you?

2. Read Matthew 5:16; Philippians 4:8–9. Talk (or write) about how these verses are personal for you. In what ways do you respond to God's love? How are these personal and specific to you?

3. Ask God to translate His love into your daily habits of service, creation, reflection, and expression. Pray for His Spirit to give you spiritual nourishment that you digest and use to strengthen your actions.

This Week

Look for ways that the powerful love of your Savior is reflected in your life, in your actions, in your faith, and in the transformation of your soul. Write about what you see God doing in your life and how you are learning to trust Him.

Pray

Dear Jesus, illuminate my life with Your example of humble service and living out Your love. Change me, Holy Spirit, so my life reflects Your love. Amen.

DAY 24

THE OTHER PART OF THE SABBATH

Come to Me, all who labor and are heavy laden, and I will give you rest. Take My yoke upon you, and learn from Me, for I am gentle and lowly in heart, and you will find rest for your souls. For My yoke is easy, and My burden is light. (Matthew 11:28–30)

My husband is a technology consultant. I'm not exactly sure what he does, but he knows a whole lot about computers and how to get them to do what we need them to do.

He's also really good at fixing things—including my old headphones that don't connect, printers that won't cooperate, and wireless routers that cannot keep up with the strain of all our devices. When anything tech-related in our house stops working, we go to Mike.

He has the same advice for anyone with a device or appliance that has an electrical problem: turn it off for a couple of minutes. Then turn it back on. *Magic.*

And you know what? This trick almost always works for tablets, and for toddlers, and for refrigerators. The trick of turning-off-and-back-on also works for you.

This spiritual practice of rest is the other part of worship. When you rest, you turn off your striving, your hustle, and your control.

Think about the story of Jesus and the thunderstorm in Mark 4:35–41. Remember the scene? All of the disciples were freaking out about the storm that was tossing the boat back and forth. They were afraid for their lives and for their livelihood—since they were fishermen who needed this boat in order to work.

And Jesus took a nap. Rain and chaos surrounded them, and Jesus, the only one who could do something about the storm, slept. He was peaceful.

When the disciples woke Jesus up, He first solved the problem. Then He talked with them about what had happened. Why had they freaked out? Calming that crazy storm had impressed the disciples. In that moment, they learned a little more about who Jesus was. Everything was under His control, including the weather, and including any other terrifying chaos they could imagine. And He was peaceful. He had been *sleeping.*

Don't you love this story of Jesus modeling rest to His disciples and to us? Doesn't a nap, out on the stormy sea, surrounded by a loud storm, sound like the most thrilling kind of rest? If your body and your mind are able to turn off for a few minutes for complete release, then you are definitely trusting that someone else is taking care of you.

Can you trust God in this same way? Can you close your eyes, right now, and relax into His powerful love? Can you take a deep breath and melt into the rocking comfort of a Savior who loves you?

As part of your worship, God gives you permission to go ahead and turn off for a bit. Take an emotional nap. Truly refresh with complete quiet. Be still. Forget the chaos of this world. You can't control it anyway. The Holy Spirit is covering you with the deep comfort and peace that surpasses understanding.

God is also giving you permission to go ahead and help someone else. Sure, we can sit around and watch football on a Sunday afternoon. We can also give a neighbor a hand with some yard work or make a pot of chili for a busy family or do something else we're good at that will help someone. This kind of work isn't part of our day job, and it isn't just unplugging and sitting still. But it *is* refreshing to take our minds off our own stormy sea and offer others a little rest from their crazy life. And it's one of the ways we can share God's love with others.

Completely relaxed and refreshed in your faith, you can better see ways to serve Him and better receive His love. You can worship Him with deep trust.

For Today

1. What is your story about needing rest? How can you tell when your body and mind have grown weary and need a break? What about when your soul needs rest? In seasons during which it's really hard for you to take a break, what's at the root of that struggle? How is rest part of worship?

2. Read Romans 4:5; Colossians 2:16–17. Scripture reveals what the Old Testament laws mean in light of Jesus and His sacrifice for us. Think about the idea of rest in the context of the Third Commandment, "Remember the Sabbath day, to keep it holy" (Exodus 20:8). Remember that the Israelites had worked as slaves seven days a week, so a day of rest was a gift to them from the Lord. What about for us? How is rest a gift for us also?

3. Read Ecclesiastes 3:1–8 as a prayer. Consider what wisdom is here for us regarding the rhythms we need as women and as Christians. As you pray these words, pause after each line and thank God for a time He's given you each of these seasons. Breathe in and out and tell the Holy Spirit how grateful you are for each of these times He has been with you, giving you this distinct season.

Challenge!

In Leviticus 25:10–11, God teaches His people to consecrate every fiftieth year as the Year of Jubilee. The practice of jubilee was about freeing slaves, returning land, and canceling debts.

The Year of Jubilee was about the Israelites returning home to their families.

How has the time of COVID been a Year of Jubilee for you? What hustle and busy-ness has COVID taken out of your schedule? How has this time of reconnection with your home and family changed you? Did this reset help you see how you might have turned work or kids into gods in your life? What deeper rest does God offer in jubilee, with His mandate to return to home and "reset"?

For today, be intentional about a return to your home and to your family. What is one way you can rest from the pressure of the world? What does your family need right now? How can you be present for that need? How can you connect and *rest* with your family?

Most important, how does this practice of rest show you the deeper peace that you have in your Savior, Jesus? Ask the Holy Spirit to fill you with faith to more fully and deeply rest in the love of your heavenly Father.

Pray

**Heavenly Father, refresh me with the Holy Spirit.
When I wear myself out, help me to trust that You
are true rest, dear Lord. As I worship You today, give
me true rest. In Jesus' name, I pray. Amen.**

DAY 25

WHEN GOD MAKES SOMETHING HAPPEN

For by Him all things were created, in heaven and on earth, visible and invisible, whether thrones or dominions or rulers or authorities—all things were created through Him and for Him. (Colossians 1:16)

Twenty years ago, when my first book was published, I learned a valuable lesson that has carried me through countless writing projects: I am in charge of the quantity; God is in charge of the quality.

In other words, I will show up to write every single morning at five. I will pour out thoughts, ideas, poems, stories, and research. I will work at it as hard as I can. I will be faithful, vigilant, and prayerful. I will rely on Scripture and even fight for the work of the Lord. And I will not worry about what it is becoming.

God is in charge of that.

In the end, all the glory belongs to God because He has given me the work of writing to do. And He will use my work to bring glory to Himself.

Over the years, I have forgotten this lesson more times than I can count, and it's always disastrous when I do. I'm not in charge of the quality or how my work is received. I am in charge of making sure I create it.

There have been times that I have wrongly believed that if I re-create what another writer has done, I will also re-create her popularity. Or I have focused so much on the beautiful product that will set the world on fire that I get bogged down in the process. My plans for success overwhelm the fragile art, and I give up.

But no matter how much I want to try to control what happens to my efforts and no matter what my vision is, God is the one who uses it for His good, when and how He chooses.

From what I can tell, this happens to a lot of us. When we make something, we want control over all of it—the ideas, the process, the ways the world will love it, the big paychecks, and the glory. When we take our eyes off the work God has given us and focus instead on our vision and goals, we have lost our purpose.

Consider a different way.

In Exodus, Moses described the story of the Israelites building the tabernacle, and it is just the very best do-it-yourself story you've ever heard. This whole community showed up and came together to create a stunning space to worship the Lord.

God's plans for the tabernacle were intentional and thought out to the tiniest detail. He selected skilled workers and "showed" them the building and its design. Every stitch, casting, and sculpture these artisans created was accomplished because God provided the raw materials and the people and the plan. But if these chosen artisans hadn't followed the plan to perfection, they would have had to do it all over again. In any case, this was God's plan. The laborers honored Him when they showed up to execute it. And the tabernacle worked because they focused on communicating to God's people the ultimate plan of salvation.

Read the beautiful words of Exodus 35:30–35:

> Then Moses said to the people of Israel, "See, the LORD has called by name Bezalel the son of Uri, son of Hur, of the tribe of Judah; and He has filled him with the Spirit of God, with skill, with intelligence, with knowledge, and with all crafts-manship, to devise artistic designs, to work in gold and silver and bronze, in cutting stones for setting, and in carving wood, for work in every skilled craft. And He has inspired him to teach, both him and Oholiab the son of Ahisamach of the tribe of Dan. He has filled them with skill to do every sort of work done by an engraver or by a designer or by an embroiderer in blue and purple and scarlet yarns and fine twined linen, or by a weaver—by any sort of workman or skilled designer.

Think about this: did God fill these workers with the Spirit of God (v. 31) because He needed them to be creative? Did He give them skills to make beautiful things because He needed the temple to be stunning, with blue, purple, and scarlet yarns and fine twisted linen? Of course not. These artists had the urge to create a beautiful tabernacle, and they did just that. And God blessed their art and efforts with skill, intelligence, knowledge, and craftsmanship. They showed up and etched the metal and embroidered the silk, and they constructed a gorgeous worship space, intent on their work and concerned with the end result.

This tent would last for the next five hundred years as the most sacred, beautiful worship space. A *tent* that these skilled craftsmen created and freely gave everything to make. They were not obsessed with whether anyone would fully appreciate their sacrifice or what the critics would say. They were tasked with showing up every day, and the Holy Spirit was in charge of blessing the space to become the hallowed place for all God's people to congregate and worship and receive Him.

Remember this when you are trying to make a new thing. You can't dictate how God will use it. Part of the vulnerability and thrill of creating something to honor God is the wonder of not knowing what will happen.

Trust that God is not indifferent or oblivious to what you are doing. Instead, know that He is intimately involved in the whole process and exactly how it unfolds. The people who showed up are the exact ones who needed to be there. The time that it happened was just when it should have. The words you spoke are the ones that needed to be said.

There is no right or wrong way to accomplish your work— there is faith and confidence that God will bless the work of your hands. There is the message of Romans 8:28 and the truth that God will use all things to His glory.

So often, we think that His glory will look like lots of money, social media followers, or fame. After all, that's what glory looks like for us humans. Then, when a project doesn't end in a hundred new members or a glowing neon sign of obvious success, we write it off as a failure.

But how can you and I know what quality or longevity God has woven into any of it? Remember, you are in charge of the quantity. Show up. Do the capital campaign. Record the podcast. Write all the words.

Then, detach yourself from the success or the failure. You simply cannot know what might unfold in this generation or in the next. You can't monetize what spiritual fruit might grow in the fertile ground of the souls of other people. You can't guess or predict how magnificently God will bless your efforts, in the most unbelievable and unforeseen ways.

For Today

1. What have you created or wanted to create? Tell or write down a list of what you would like to make. Now explore where your control might be getting in your way. Write an encouraging note to yourself with this reminder: "I'm in charge of the quantity; God decides the quality." Hang that note someplace where you'll see it the next time you're tempted to burden your creativity with expectation.

2. Read Colossians 3:23–24. How is creating like working for the Lord? What inheritance do you receive? How is this serving the Lord?

3. A challenge when we're creating something that gives glory to God is to resist the urge to take control in order to achieve our own vision. It's one thing to be a solo artist. But when we agree to a specific effort, like the tabernacle workers did, we are accountable. When we join a project or engage in a ministry, we agree to keep the goals and overall plan in mind. Remember that a creative endeavor might be using your gifts to point another person to Jesus. That's no longer solo work. Pray for God to remove your personal expectations and lean into confidence in Him instead. Pray that He equips you for the end goal: to make known Jesus, our Redeemer and Savior.

Challenge!

Today is the day! Make something that you know will bless someone else. Record yourself singing or playing an instrument.

Bake a loaf of bread. Paint a picture of a favorite place and give it to someone who needs beauty right now. Lean into your curiosity about making rather than your fear about how it will turn out. Make yourself a promise that you will be open to what God does with this thing. Maybe it was simply to give you joy, or maybe it blesses someone else on their journey to know Jesus. Promise to send yourself a text in one week with a recap of how God used this creation in His ministry to the world.

Pray

Heavenly Father, holy Creator, thank You for this beautiful world You have made. Help me to join in by allowing Your Spirit to renew my faith. Remove my fear and replace it with trust in You. In Jesus' name, I pray. Amen.

DAY 26

STUCK

For we ourselves were once foolish, disobedient, led astray, slaves to various passions and pleasures, passing our days in malice and envy, hated by others and hating one another. But when the goodness and loving kindness of God our Savior appeared, He saved us, not because of works done by us in righteousness, but according to His own mercy, by the washing of regeneration and renewal of the Holy Spirit. (Titus 3:3–5)

I am smack-dab middle-aged, and I've been noticing something. This time of life seems to be the point when a woman's mental furniture gets stuck in one layout. This feels like the age when we become rigid.

This is the age that many of us start to need glasses. This seems like a metaphor to me because, at this point in our lives, we start to lose some perspective. Our minds and bodies start to look for comfort and routine. We become inflexible. Pessimistic. Even suspicious.

What can we do about this? We can rely on God for inspiration and help. We can look to our value as redeemed daughters to know that we are loved.

And we can wear the glasses of faith—that is, rejecting fear and instead leaning one-hundred percent on the work of the Holy Spirit to keep rejuvenating each of us with trust in the Lord and conviction to live a rich life in Him.

What does this look like?

For me, it means I don't want to give up being hopeful and trusting to become hardened and skeptical. I don't want to lose my sense of awe, hope, and confidence that God can redeem any situation. I don't want to stop creating or risking so I can become very safe and comfortable. I want to take chances, and I want to be part of all the moments of this one, beautiful life.

I want to be so filled up with the Holy Spirit and the gifts of love, joy, peace, patience, kindness, and gentleness that I overflow them to the people in my world. I want to be pliable to the work God is doing in my soul, constantly putting on new pairs of glasses and letting God rearrange all my mental furniture into crazy patterns to fit whatever new season He wants me to tackle.

What about you?

Do you want to take God at His word in Romans 12:2? Paul describes the work of the Holy Spirit with these words: "Do not be conformed to this world, but be transformed by the renewal of your mind, that by testing you may discern what is the will of God, what is good and acceptable and perfect."

Don't you want to be transformed by the renewal of your mind? Do you see how the letdowns of this world could harden you into a person you never wanted to become? Maybe you've felt this happening in seasons that were really challenging.

Maybe you've sold out so much of what you know, deep in your spirit, just to follow the really bad advice of the world. Maybe you've tried to take care of things yourself, and that has made you cynical.

Or maybe you have lost connection with those you love. You might feel guilty about the thousands of times you've felt the urge to call, text, or visit a friend who is hurting. But then you've gotten in your own head about how awkward that would be, and instead of trusting God's Word to equip you through the hard thing, you avoid it altogether. Instead, you scroll, scroll, scroll through mindless things that numb that nudge, until this urge to connect with someone passes and you feel safe again.

Or consider the times you've passed the homeless, or the clearly hurting, and not helped. Think of the millions of chances you've been presented to give more, love more freely, show mercy to someone who is absolutely going through life's wringer. Instead of trusting the Spirit to equip you, you've rationalized it all in your mind. You've justified your apathy and shushed the call of the Spirit by allowing your mind to suppress it with a cascade of reasons. After all, complicating your day to help another doesn't make logical sense, right?

Yeah, me too. All of it.

I don't want to get stuck in these patterns. Do you? Can you see how the world has arranged your mental furniture for you to believe that perfectionism and control are the ways to feel secure? Do you notice that you've been conformed to this world in ways that make you stuck in your own sin patterns? Do you cringe at the days when you acted against what you knew was God's will and the Holy Spirit's nudging in order to do what was easier, what would get you more likes, what would make you feel safe?

I suspect it happens like this. We give up listening to the small, countercultural voice of the Spirit, and we settle more and more into what the world tells us is comfortable. It's a long slog of relying on ourselves, of not allowing God to renew our minds with His Spirit, of becoming cynical that God is too detached from our problems, and that the Bible doesn't really apply to the issues of the world today. Instead of trusting Him and His Word for us, we accept that the world, these thoughts, and the weakness of this flesh are what life is all about.

To be clear, this can happen at any age for any woman. More important, you never have to give into it. You do not have to accept the sloppy lies being served to you. You can live a life that is open to exploring instead of a mindless routine of thin contentment. You can live in God's fresh perspective of hope instead of the negativity of twenty-four-hour news. You can have real connection—the kind that's unscripted, awkward, vulnerable, and very real—rather than another dozen (or another million) posts about fashion trends and kids' dance recitals and low-grade, mean comments about whole groups of people. And, honestly, you do that by inwardly digesting His Word. It's personal for you. Even if you read the same psalm or chapter a dozen times, each time you read it, it speaks to each season of your life in a new and renewing way.

Your body will become old and tired and lose its physical energy. But not your spirit—God will keep renewing it with His beautiful new life and create something fresh in you every minute of every day.

You can have a free, beautiful, reckless, real life with your Savior and never, ever settle for less.

For Today

1. Talk (or write) about seasons when bitterness, complacency, or cynicism have taken over your mind. In what ways was the Holy Spirit also working in your life? How did you see this?

2. Read Colossians 3:10. Consider your life right now. How can you put on a new self—one that's in the image of your Creator? What about your mindset, daily routine, relationships, and life right now needs transforming? How can these changes be from the Holy Spirit?

3. Is there an adventure to which God is calling you that doesn't make sense? How is rearranging your mental furniture new and scary? Pray about how God is moving in your spirit. Ask God to lead you. Then, turn off your phone, close this book, go for a walk, and contemplate what He has told you in His Word. Feel the faith the Holy Spirit is renewing in you, and then embrace a new perspective.

Challenge!

Take thirty minutes of uninterrupted quiet time. Imagine yourself decades older. Visit with this older, wiser version of yourself. What message does she have for you? How does she carry herself? How does she interact with you? Are there people around? Talk with her about a situation you are struggling with and tell her how you feel. Write what you see in her and how you can be more like that right now. Ask God to show this to you.

Pray

Lord, please inspire me to see my life, my relationships, my mind, and my gifts through Your eyes.
Give me the perspective to see the work Your Spirit
is urging me toward all the time. Amen.

DAY 27

HOW IT FEELS TO FORGIVE SOMEONE FOR REAL

And Peter said to them, "Repent and be baptized every one of you in the name of Jesus Christ for the forgiveness of your sins, and you will receive the gift of the Holy Spirit." (Acts 2:38)

I have written Bible studies about forgiveness for two decades, and I keep learning more and more about how true forgiveness works. Probably others could learn it faster, but I do love to analyze forgiveness: how do we have the power to forgive? Where is it described in the Bible? Where do you see yourself in how God describes forgiveness?

I *think* so much about the theology of forgiveness—and yet I don't always actually do it. Because forgiveness can be awkward. And a grudge sometimes feels so good to carry. Also, I often feel like I don't really deserve forgiveness, and then I get too stuck in that shame to forgive others.

The crazy news I didn't fully grasp until now is that true forgiveness can't come from the flesh, mind, or ego. Forgiveness is something God works in us.

Over the past year, God has taken me through this transformation from a head-centered Christian to a Spirit-empowered believer. I can see now how I was trusting my mind to do the impossible, to do something it was never able to. I was asking my pride and ego to think my way into giving full, humble grace to myself and other people.

When someone hurt my feelings, I felt the familiar pinch of anger and hurt pride. To avoid that emotional pain, I didn't allow myself to feel it. Instead, I thought about it. Constantly. Then I beat myself up for thinking about it so much. I made myself feel guilty for being angry and unable to forgive.

This, folks, is what we call being in your own head. Trying to do spiritual work by the power of my own mind is like thinking really super hard about a five-mile run, and then marking it off my list as done. Ha. As if.

What changed is when I started praying for a different understanding of forgiveness. "Come, Holy Spirit; wash through me. Take away the old me. No more bitterness and anger. Lord, fill me with Your goodness. Get rid of the old me, and create a clean heart in me. Daily, repeatedly, continuously. Transform me into a person like Christ. Fill me with His love."

I love the way Paul describes this transformation in Galatians 2:20: "I have been crucified with Christ. It is no longer I who live, but Christ who lives in me. And the life I now live in the flesh I live by faith in the Son of God, who loved me and gave Himself for me."

To be crucified with Christ is really a death that happens in your soul, the death of sin. The old, sinful self must die, and then you are filled with God's love and forgiveness. No more grudge. No more revenge. No more shame about how you do not deserve forgiveness.

This isn't me doing this just by thinking it—it's absolutely the Spirit's power that washes through me and makes me new in Christ Jesus. No more struggling for control now, just peaceful love and generosity for the other person.

This is what happened when you became a child of God, when the water literally washed over you and God's Holy Word was spoken over you. You don't deserve this forgiveness or do anything to earn it, but it is yours because you're baptized. This is the work of the Holy Spirit for you. And this happens every day, all the time; not just that one time when you were held up to the font.

True, spiritual forgiveness can feel a little physically painful and has even been described as a violent act. It's no wonder I avoided it for so long. The physical sensation of anger, pride, and bitterness dying in my soul is uncomfortable. I have to acknowledge my own sin, but it's like I'm afraid there will be a deep black hole there.

But there never is. My soul is covered in the softest velvet of joy and inexpressible peace.

Maybe you already know this process of real forgiveness. If you have also experienced this spiritual process, then you know the relief that comes with really letting someone else off the hook the same way Jesus let you off the hook when He was hanging on the cross. Maybe you learned long ago that this before-and-after of Baptism and then faith is completely transformative to the way you understood grace as a free gift.

This is the daily drowning of yourself and your pride and your ego. This work of forgiveness and sanctification is the process of becoming more Christlike. This beautiful, transformative, invigorating, life-giving change is the work of the Holy Spirit in your life. This is beautiful grace.

Best of all, it is available to you right now.

For Today

1. Forgiveness can become about how your mental furniture is arranged. You might have been taught by your parents that forgiveness requires a lot of guilt. Or you might believe that some people are not worthy of forgiveness. What did you learn about forgiveness from your family? Did it turn out to be true?

2. Read Matthew 18:21–22. What point is Jesus making about forgiveness? Is it something you can measure or analyze?

3. Pray for your enemies (Mark 11:25), that God would help you to forgive them. Go ahead and pray right now. Tell God about three people against whom you hold bitterness that you wish you could release—and then ask God to help you.

Challenge!

Experience a moment of the Spirit's power as you forgive someone right now. Sit in silence and imagine this person who has hurt you. Sit with the memory of what he or she did to you. Feel the anger, the hurt, and the grief of what this person took from you. Don't squirm away from this task. Experience the full range of the physical repulsion of this memory.

Now, ask God to help you release this hurt right now. Picture the day you were baptized and water was poured over your head as the pastor spoke the words of forgiveness. Realize that this flow of forgiveness is constant. Can you feel the anger leaving you? Are you experiencing this lightening? That's forgiveness. Repeat as often as necessary. Say, "I forgive you" aloud. Pray for God to continue this work in you. Write about the process and what changes come from this prayer.

Pray

Dear Jesus, thank You for dying on the cross so
I could be forgiven and so I could forgive others.
Please, my dear Savior, give me the love, the power,
and the strength to receive forgiveness from You and
to extend it to others. Ignite this transformation in
my soul through the Holy Spirit. Amen.

DAY 28

GOD SPEAKS TO YOU

Having gifts that differ according to the grace given to us, let us use them: if prophecy, in proportion to our faith; if service, in our serving; the one who teaches, in his teaching; the one who exhorts, in his exhortation; the one who contributes, in generosity; the one who leads, with zeal; the one who does acts of mercy, with cheerfulness. (Romans 12:6–8)

One of my earliest memories was sitting cross-legged on the asphalt parking lot of my preschool, listening to two second graders at our small school as they passionately sold us paper clothes for our Barbie dolls.

Their names were Stephanie and John and they had been hard at work creating a little business. While we little girls played with our Barbie dolls at recess, Stephanie and John were drawing, coloring, and cutting little T-shirts, shorts, and dresses that were perfectly sized to our dolls. One day, they gathered all of us together and told us how we could buy tons of cool new outfits for our dolls! Only a quarter for an outfit!

Their presentation mesmerized me. Both Stephanie and John were so passionate about how these clothes were brilliant and just what every Barbie needed. I could feel their excitement about the little paper cowboy boots that we could buy and slip over our dolls' feet. Their exclamations of "perfect fit!" "so cute!" and "one of a kind!" transfixed me. I went home, dumped out my piggy bank, and bought all the clothes.

I remember this moment so well because it was the first time I experienced the sensation of how fascinating I have always found a convincing speaker.

The next time I remember this feeling was in middle school—a particularly hard time in my personal history—while listening to a guest speaker who came to convince us to stay away from drugs. This was the 1980s, and we were supposed to "just say no." As this truly gifted speaker ranted to us about the dangers of cocaine and marijuana, I sat in the bleachers, absolutely spellbound. There was that feeling again. His charisma and passion spoke deep into my soul, and by the time he reached the apex of his talk about us kids being the future, I was openly weeping with emotion. I felt his message so hard. (By the way, crying at motivational speakers did zero to up my coolness game with the other twelve-year-olds.)

In college, I was often the only one of my friends who went to hear guest lecturers. If they were giving a sort-of TED Talk (long before actual TED Talks) about how to make a difference in the world or how to share our faith, I would always cry. For the next few days, I would carry with me the passion and conviction of the speaker.

Then I became a teacher, where I could stand in front of my students and motivate them to learn by speaking about the subject at hand. And since I am a Lutheran school teacher, I could live out my love for God and His Word in my day job. But it was at a faculty retreat that I found my voice. I volunteered to give a devotion to the group. My job was to speak about Ephesians 4:11–12 and give a ten-minute pep talk to a hundred or so weary teachers. As I took the microphone and started to talk to my peers about how God calls teachers to share His love with students, a sensation washed over me. The faculty leaned in, applauded, and a couple of teachers even wrote me notes about my message.

I realized then that this is what I'm supposed to do with my life. I was made for this. I want to tell the world about God's love. I want to share my passion for Jesus. I want to equip people and build up the Body of Christ.

That undeniable feeling that had sparked in my soul for years, every time I heard a speaker? Ah, it all made sense now. That was a nudge from the Holy Spirit.

That first devotion to the group of teachers was twenty-five years ago, and I've had the opportunity to speak hundreds of times since. I love it. Even during the times when there are problems with the tech (and there are always problems with the tech), or when I'm tired, or when the event falls right in the middle of a long list of other commitments, or when it's for high school kids (who hate being forced to sit through anything), I still love it.

Some friends feel this way about singing or playing an instrument. For me, those activities are hard and awkward, and when I'm doing any of them, I can feel every aspect of self-consciousness and fear. It's speaking and writing that make me feel alive, that engage my energy. These are the particular gifts God has given me, and I've felt that passion zinging throughout my life. What's more, I see on people's faces that they are listening to my message and often, after I've given a speech, they tell me how I've helped them see God at work in their lives and that their faith is strengthened.

God has given me other jobs: my vocations as wife, mother, teacher, daughter, citizen. With those vocations comes all the stuff of everyday life and responsibility. To be sure, all that work can feel mundane sometimes. But I find passion here too. Joy at the knowledge that God put me with these people. Peace that we're together. God has equipped me for regular daily life too.

What about you? What has God given you to do? What passions can you trace through your life? What have you always been curious about? What are you doing when you lose track of time? What have you always loved, since the first time you experienced it? How did you know that this was different than other things?

It can be hard to hear God's voice amid so many others. Your vocation might feel muddled at times. It might even feel difficult.

For this reason, spending time with Him is so important. Rest in His Word. Pray. Hear the Gospel proclaimed. Read (or sing) a hymn. Receive the Lord's Supper. And listen. Journal about what He's saying to you. Carve out lots of time to pay attention to what He might want you to do to serve Him and help others.

The gift of the Holy Spirit is to share God's love with the world. Like any gift, you did nothing to earn it and do nothing to keep it. You don't have to feel guilty or self-righteous because His gift is the way God equips you to spread His Word to the very ends of the earth. Instead, see yourself as one part of a

Body that is made up of others who are as gifted, as equipped as you so they can do their part in God's kingdom on earth too.

Go forth to equip the saints for the work of ministry. Let's do the Lord's work and build up the Body of Christ.

For Today

1. Some spiritual gifts are evangelism, hospitality, wisdom, giving, teaching, and leading. Which of these light up your soul? Talk about (or write about) these things in your life. Which spiritual gift do you believe you have? Where have you seen this in your personal history?

2. Read 1 Corinthians 12:4, 7–11; Ephesians 4:11–13; Romans 12:4–8; 1 Peter 4:10–11. What is the important message of all of these verses? (Look especially at 1 Corinthians 12:4.)

3. In your prayer journal or in your daily prayers this week, ask God to show you the gifts that the Holy Spirit has given you. How can you use these gifts to serve Him in new ways? Be alert to the Holy Spirit's guidance as you pray.

Challenge!

Write down one spiritual gift you think you might have. (Remember, according to the Bible, spiritual gifts might include prophecy, service, teaching, exhortation, giving, leadership, mercy, wisdom, knowledge, faith, healing, apostleship, helping, administration, and evangelism.)

Below where you wrote your spiritual gift, write ways that God has given you chances in the past to use this spiritual gift in your home or church or community—among your family and friends and co-workers to point others to Jesus and to glorify God. After you've written about one or two of those chances, write one or two opportunities you have to use this gift *right now.* Then, make a call or send an email or a text about how you might use this gift. Can you serve on a committee or board, join the church choir, or write a devotion to share online? Before you go to sleep tonight, make sure you have taken this one step about a way to use this gift. Tomorrow, follow up about the opportunity and find a use for your unique spiritual gift.

Pray

Lord, show me Your ways. Give me eyes to see who You are and what You want me to do. Give me faith, Lord. Help me to use my gifts to serve You. In the power of Jesus' name, I pray. Amen.

CONCLUSION: TO THE ENDS OF THE EARTH

Brothers, I do not consider that I have made it my own. But one thing I do: forgetting what lies behind and straining forward to what lies ahead, I press on toward the goal for the prize of the upward call of God in Christ Jesus. (Philippians 3:13–14)

A couple of years ago, we were living in a different city—in Katy, Texas. We were part of a Christian school that we had invested in since it opened. Our church was like an extended part of our family. Also, our actual family (both my parents and Mike's) had moved to live in Katy too. We shared our lives with them and always saw them at church and all our kids' activities. Our neighbors were like our family as well. Mike and one neighbor had started a company together. We had weathered through and cleaned up from several storms together—both actual hurricanes and the personal storms that come from living shoulder to shoulder.

This was our community—our people—and we loved it.

And yet . . .

One day, a friend commented about being at our school for ten years, and then she said, "Ten years is a good time to reflect. Is there still work you need to do here, or are your gifts not needed as much anymore?" Without thinking, a punch to my gut answered the question, and I just knew: my gifts weren't needed as much anymore. Not in this place, at least.

That gut-punch got me thinking—who was our family *really*? One of our dreams had been to have all our kids in the same school. That wasn't possible in Katy, but what if we moved to Friendswood, where they could? And then I could teach at our Lutheran school, something I wanted to do again. The vision of all that, plus being closer to my hometown of Galveston, got Mike and me asking all kinds of questions about what our family needed in this new season of life.

But we didn't do anything about it at first. Instead, I began to pay attention and to pray. Were there really enough good reasons to uproot our family? Were we just going through a phase? What about contentment? What about blooming where you're planted?

This time, we had a different conviction. The things that had defined our family for so long didn't define us anymore. Our goals had become more centered on ministry and sharing Christ, and we couldn't find our footing where we were.

I was spending lots of quiet time in prayer, and I kept hearing a confirmation that this season had fulfilled its purpose. I craved the quiet time to hear all of that. I journaled through it and contemplated and grieved the tremendous loss of leaving our people, our town, our community, and our family.

If you've ever moved, you know what I mean about trying to decide what's best for your family. This change was hard because we had grown around the city of Katy like a tree grows around a sidewalk. Sometimes I would forget we were leaving, and then I would remember, and the idea of it seemed so inconvenient and weird that I would panic. These people, places, little communities, stores, and restaurants were what made us the Hergenrader family. Was it some kind of twisted self-sabotage to leave it?

Slowly, another thing was happening. Coincidences. Doors opened three or four at a time.

And yet. It was a leap of faith to move to another city with no safety net and no promises. Except that God would be with us.

Over and over, ideas about life in Friendswood would pop into my head. When I followed up on the ideas, the plans worked out. Could we buy this house? Yes. Boom. Done. Does this congregation offer what we are looking for and also provide us with ways to serve God and the community? Sure does. How about going back to teaching? Here's a job offer from that Lutheran school. God was blessing this.

In truth, leaving Katy and moving to Friendswood meant I had to let go of an identity. This revealed all kinds of idols I didn't know I had. Our beautiful home, our status as beloved children and grandchildren to our parents, and trustworthy neighbors who had built a life around our shared day-to-day rhythm. I had turned those wonderful blessings into little idols.

Letting go of them was so painful. At the same time, we were learning a much bigger lesson: we were not the life we had created; we were followers of Christ, and through Him, God would provide for us wherever we went.

Seasons such as this can hold an enormous sense of loss. But for us, the move turned out to be a necessary sifting of our lives. Our schedules, egos, and identities had become so bloated with who we were to everyone else that we needed this next chapter to strip away some of those false securities.

We emerged from this transition with a deeper faith than before. We were lonely and afraid and anxious about whether we had done the right thing, but God filled in those gaps with the assurance of who He is in our lives. Dear friends, God provided us with so much abundance that I cannot even believe we doubted our move would work. We have been able to shift our focus from who we were in our community to who we are in God's kingdom and how we can serve Him and others with our gifts and abilities.

Perhaps the Lord has sifted your life too. As your heavenly Father has moved you from one chapter to the next, you discovered what you didn't need anymore. You learned that your true identity as a follower of Christ was the only one that mattered.

Perhaps, like us, you learned that it was our Lord taking care of you.

It had been Him the whole time.

For Today

1. It's so easy to get wound up in the identity of making people happy. Success feels like everything when you're in an ego-soaked world. But there is another reality for you away from these roles. What roles and identities do you feel too attached to right now?

2. Read Acts 1:8. What does this mean about where and what God is calling you to do? What does this mean to you right now? Where does God want you to share His love with the world?

3. Name your deepest prayer right now. Just write it out. What is the thing you really want God to do in your life? Now, list the things happening in your life that show God is answering this prayer. Listen to what God is saying to you right now. If you doodle a letter to yourself from God, what does it say? Through His Word, God speaks to our souls all the time; what is He saying to you right now?

Challenge!

Quit something today. You probably even know what it is—the volunteer role you're not really suited for, the task you've outgrown but keep doing, the relationship with the person who makes you feel bad about yourself, or the gym membership that you thought would make you work out but only makes you feel guilty.

Here's how to do it: ask God to be with you without this part of your identity (He totally will be), and then leave it behind. Ask Him to show you how to honor Him with some new endeavor.

Ah, doesn't that feel lighter?

Pray

O Lord, be clear in my life about who You want me to be and what You want me to do. Help me to follow Your lead. Amen.

Epilogue: Breathe

Then the LORD God formed the man of dust from the ground and breathed into his nostrils the breath of life, and the man became a living creature. (Genesis 2:7)

And when He had said this, He breathed on them and said to them, "Receive the Holy Spirit." (John 20:22)

Welcome to the end of your four-week study. Welcome to the end of this season and the start of the next. Welcome to a lifetime of new habits.

Thank you for showing up and trusting God in this process of spiritual transformation. Thank you for reading, discussing, learning, opening up, trying, failing, and trying again. What a month! I truly hope you've found new gems of joy, peace, love, expectation, and inspiration to create that are hidden in the folds of your life and given to you through the Holy Spirit. I hope you've found exactly what you were looking for. I hope you understand God the Holy Spirit in a new and exciting way, that His breath of life is spoken over you in the Sacraments and in the preaching and teaching of God's Word for you. I hope you look out through the new pair of glasses—the security of faith—that you received in your Baptism.

As you go forward, dear friend, let the Holy Spirit live in your beautiful soul and inspire and guide you, in all of your ways and in all of your days.

Through it all, breathe.

Breathe, dear one, as you find what you are passionate to make and what you love to do.

Jeremiah had a burning fire in his bones to share God's Word (Jeremiah 20:9). This was his purpose.

What about you? Have you found the treasures, talents, and gifts that God has given you? What fire is in your bones? Does holding in your fire make you grow weary?

Because of Jesus, we have a firm foundation for identity as we grow and understand our life *in Him*. We are a new creation *in Him*. So breathe out new creations. Do it all—write the silly poem, the prayerful song, the brilliant painting, the funny T-shirt, the book of devotions. There is no creation police. You have just as much right to create as anyone else does. Do your thing. Here is your permission slip to find your fire:

> If I say, "I will not mention Him, or speak any more in His name," there is in my heart as it were a burning fire shut up in my bones, and I am weary with holding it in, and I cannot. (Jeremiah 20:9)

Again—breathe! Let the fruit of the Holy Spirit grow in your life and change your relationships.

The Spirit breathes much-needed nutrients to this fruit. Our world needs it.

As we are all learning, we become more connected than we could ever imagine. When you show the fruit of the Spirit to your kids, they share the fruit of the Spirit with mine.

This inspired life is one of community. Be right here, fully present and showing the world what true kindness and humbleness look like. It looks like compassionate hearts, harmony, and one Body of Christ. It looks like hope and peace that come only from faith in the One who joins you to Himself.

> Put on then, as God's chosen ones, holy and beloved, compassionate hearts, kindness, humility, meekness, and patience, bearing with one another and, if one has a complaint against another, forgiving each other; as the Lord has forgiven you, so you also must forgive. And above all these put on love, which binds everything together in perfect harmony. And let the peace of Christ rule in your hearts, to which indeed you were called in one body. And be thankful. Let the word of Christ dwell in you richly, teaching and admonishing one another in all wisdom, singing psalms and hymns and spiritual songs, with thankfulness in your hearts to God. And whatever you do, in word or deed, do everything in the name of the Lord Jesus, giving thanks to God the Father through Him. (Colossians 3:12–17)

Take deeper breaths now as you live out forgiveness from the Spirit—even for yourself. Especially for yourself. Christ is in you.

Yes, you keep messing up. Your to-do list has had the same three need-to-do! tasks on it for weeks now. You thought you would be really good at something, but it turns out you're not and you can't shake the shame. You're overdue for your dental cleaning. You spent too much money online shopping, and the returns are sitting there like a pile of shame.

You're too busy to keep in touch with those you truly love, and you waste hours scrolling through pictures of people you went to high school with and don't know anymore. And are you really paying for that gym membership you are not even using? Loser.

Guess what? Me too. I've also done all of this. I've controlled my day to the point that I never have to leave my comfort zone. I've done everything to take care of myself and forget about love, power, or wisdom from my actual Savior.

I have gone through whole seasons of guilt, shame, and judgy-ness. I have carried around low-level disgust for those I'm supposed to love the most. I have taken credit for everything good in my life and refused to see the source of it.

All the things. And, man, when I do all of these, it all takes a toll on my soul. I'm lugging around an extra hundred pounds of bad feelings.

Breathe. You are still worthy because of your Lord Jesus Christ. In and out. Nothing can take away from you your identity as God's child.

Can that be possible? Can I be such a hot mess and also be loved and forgiven by Jesus? Can I be so disappointed in myself but also be so loved by God?

Yes. All of this. Both of these. All the time. That's the way it feels to live as both a sinner and a saint. We are all in constant need of forgiveness, and at the same time, we are totally forgiven. We're running low-grade fevers of shame, but we're also sanctified. We're looking for something to make us feel worthy, and we're constantly reminded of the miraculous work of the Holy Spirit happening right now in our souls.

> For all who are led by the Spirit of God are sons of God. For you did not receive the spirit of slavery to fall back into fear, but you have received the Spirit of adoption as sons, by whom we cry, "Abba! Father!" The Spirit Himself bears witness with our spirit that we are children of God, and if children, then heirs—heirs of God and fellow heirs with Christ, provided we suffer with Him in order that we may also be glorified with Him. (Romans 8:14–17)

Breathe. Inhale and exhale. Be present for the beautiful, breathtaking moments of this life.

> [1] The LORD is my shepherd; I shall not want.
> [2] He makes me lie down in green pastures.
> He leads me beside still waters.
> [3] He restores my soul.
> He leads me in paths of righteousness
>   for His name's sake.
> [4] Even though I walk through the valley of the
>   shadow of death,
>   I will fear no evil,

for You are with me;
>
> Your rod and Your staff,
>
> they comfort me.

⁵ You prepare a table before me
>
> in the presence of my enemies;

You anoint my head with oil;
>
> my cup overflows.

⁶ Surely goodness and mercy shall follow me
>
> all the days of my life,

and I shall dwell in the house of the LORD
>
> forever. (Psalm 23)

Breathe in the hard, awkward, wonderful moments of this one life.

Feel the inspired life of the Holy Spirit as you experience this moment. Share it with your family, and see these faces, this flesh, those eyes that are so familiar and changing with every moment (Ecclesiastes 3:11). *And breathe.*

When you sing the rich chords of hymns your people have sung for generations. Feel the memory and love that brews so much emotion that you can feel it in your throat and behind your eyes. Feel it when you sing the worship songs that light up your soul with the reminder that life is so much more (Psalm 47). *And breathe.*

When you finally say the bold, vulnerable words that need to be said and you can feel the tension leave and the Holy Spirit rush in (Jeremiah 20:9). *And breathe.*

When you stand toe-to-toe with the problem that has sparked anxiety in you a million times before—and this time, you face it. You can feel the faith and know that the power of the Holy Spirit is burning in your soul (Romans 8:11). *And breathe.*

Remember to breathe in this inspired life, my friend. This new life is grace, forgiveness, love, and transformation.

You've been created to breathe the Spirit. Never grow weary. *Keep breathing.*

For Today

1. When do you feel yourself holding your breath, spiritually or physically? Maybe it's when you're facing down some terrible anxiety. Maybe it's when you're really angry at someone and can't (or won't) forgive them. Maybe it's when scarcity pinches your finances or a friend has hurt your feelings. Also, give examples of when you feel like you can breathe easily. Where can you find breath when you feel there is none? How can your breath serve as a reminder of the Holy Spirit's work in you?

2. Look at these words from Ezekiel 37:5 again: "Thus says the Lord GOD to these bones: 'Behold, I will cause breath to enter you, and you shall live.'"

   For you, what does it mean to live—to truly live? In the next part of the scene (v. 6), the prophet witnesses the Spirit animating the dry bones. "And I will lay sinews upon you, and will cause flesh to come upon you, and cover you with skin, and put breath in you, and you shall live, and you shall know that I am the LORD."

   You also experience this same new life when you have the Holy Spirit in you. Talk about what that could look like in your life going forward. In what parts of your life do you need this? Pray for God to breathe His dynamic, divine Spirit into your soul.

3. Read Ephesians 1:3 as a prayer. Breathe in and out. Memorize Paul's words that this promise of every spiritual blessing is yours. Through the Father, Jesus

Christ, and the Holy Spirit, you belong here and you are inspired. Ask God to be the God of peace in your heart so that you may be anchored to Him, now and always.

Challenge!

Write a letter to yourself from your soul. Tell yourself what you want to remember about this month of living a more Spirit-filled life. Write about what you've learned about God's truth and His love for you. Tell yourself what you need to keep living a life inspired by the Holy Spirit. Remind yourself that God will forever give you what you need, in each breath, to live your best life in Him.

Pray

God of breath and life, fill my entire being with Your Spirit. Help me to breathe in Your love and breathe out fear. Remind me to live in Your Word, in praise to You, through prayer, and in a life of reflection. Always, Lord, keep me close to You, through the Holy Spirit. In Jesus' name, I pray. Amen.

Let it be so, forever and ever. Amen.

ANSWERS TO DAILY QUESTIONS

Day 2

1. Answers will vary but will include that most of us find our days crowded with too much information. We hold on to facts, connections, and data in hopes that it will give us peace. Scripture is different because it is oxygen for our souls—the true hope we need.

2. This passage is a picture of constantly relying on the Word of God in every part of your day. Most of us live out this kind of devotion to information from the internet, twenty-four-hour news stations, and social media. But if we made reading and memorizing Scripture a greater part of our daily lives, the power of God's Holy Word would change our souls and our minds.

Day 3

1. Answers will vary as women tell their own faith stories. Encourage discussion about times when we have found ourselves completely relying on our own abilities instead of trusting God to provide exactly the perfect timing, people, skills, and opportunities for each of our faith stories.

2. The Holy Spirit will teach you things (John 14:26); the Spirit will convict you and the world and guide you in truth (John 16:7–8, 13); the Holy Spirit allows you to witness (Acts 1:8); the Spirit guarantees your redemption and helps you to know God better (Ephesians 1:13, 17–20); the Spirit gives you eternal life and intercedes for you in prayer (Romans 8:10–11, 26–27).

Day 4

1. Answers will vary but will include stories about guilt and humiliation. Shame is painful. Because of Jesus, we are forgiven, and because of the Holy Spirit, you can live as a new creation.

2. Answers will vary but will include that through the Spirit, you have the power of spiritual healing. This cleansing transforms your understanding of yourself. Through Jesus, you are forgiven. We are holy.

Day 5

1. Answers will vary but will include that you feel disconnected from hope, afraid, numb, and are desperately searching for some relief to feel whole again. Encourage deeper responses or stories about what spiritual dehydration has looked like in your individual life.

2. God promises reconciliation, healing, and wholeness to His people. This promise is also for us. We also have the Holy Spirit, who animates our souls with the life-giving nourishment we need.

Day 6

1. Answers will vary but will include the truth that when we only read the Bible for answers, we become very focused on using it for answers. But the Bible is so much more than that. It's also a comfort and a resting place. It's also inspiration. Mostly, it is the Good News that God is living and active and caring for us.

2. John tells us plainly that there is so much more to the story. Jesus "did many other signs in the presence of the disciples, which are not written in [the Bible]" (John 20:30). God's Word is for you so we can "believe that Jesus is the Christ, the Son of God, and that by believing you may have life in His name" (John 20:31). The author of Hebrews tells us that "the Word of God is living and active" (Hebrews 4:12). The Bible shows us the absolute truth about who God is.

Day 7

1. Answers will vary but will include stories and testimonies where women have seen kindness, as well as where it is missing. Encourage stories about how radical kindness can inspire more kindness. Discussion should include the ultimate kindness that Jesus shows.

2. Patience and kindness both come from a humble spirit. True grace is full of patience and radical kindness. Jesus shows us persistent kindness, grace, and mercy.

Day 8

1. Answers will vary but may include success, money, talent, a nicer house, more friends, loving and talented children, more time and energy, and a more caring spouse.

2. God equips you for His work. He always gives you the resources, time, talent, and treasures to accomplish His work.

Day 9

1. Answers will vary and will include discussion about what we all need: to know we will be safe, that God is in control, that He loves us, and that He will take care of each one of us through eternity. Women will share stories of what these prayer answers have looked like in their lives.

2. When you pray, God gives you the Holy Spirit. Keep this in mind this week as you live out a prayer-filled life. So much good comes from prayer. He opens the door for you, and through that door is a life in which deep peace is available to you in any moment.

Day 10

1. Answers will vary but will include that we often rely on money, appearance, conforming to what others want us to be, and gossiping or manipulating others to feel better about ourselves. Life in the Spirit feels different. It's true rest, knowing that you already have everything you need. You can feel the river of that peace and love deep inside you.

2. Answers will vary but will include that life in the Spirit means regular worship, Bible study, prayer, and allowing our hearts, minds, and lives to be changed by the lavish Holy Spirit that God pours out on our lives. The fruit we produce is the fruit of the Spirit (Galatians 5:22–23). We feel like the chaff the wind blows away when we isolate ourselves from Christian community, when we don't attend worship or the Lord's Supper, and when we don't read Scripture.

Day 11

1. Answers will vary but will include that so many of us focus on a standard of perfection. We are uncomfortable when we have to face our own limitations. Creating feels hard because the results are unknown. This process requires grace for ourselves because the process means failing and starting over again.

2. In both Genesis 1:2 and Psalm 104, we read about God as the Creator and the presence of the Holy Spirit. But look at these verses. They show the opposite of cerebral life. They depict the presence and the worship of a very mysterious Creator.

Day 12

1. Answers will vary but will include stories of sickness and death, abuse, divorce, depression, and financial ruin. These traumatic experiences always change the way you see the world. Women will recount how God often uses the tragedies in our lives to rebuild our faith and our reality to see His work and strength.

2. Jesus calls the Holy Spirit "the Helper" (John 15:26). The Holy Spirit gives you God's strength, His love, and faith in His plan for you. These gifts are eternal, and understanding this life as a gift will change your entire perspective. By trusting God, you see that He will always take care of you and work all things for your good.

Day 13

1. Answers will vary but may include hot political topics of the day. Political division is constant and born out of ego. Our hope is in love in the Spirit. This love is what will soften our spirits and help us to live as one people.

2. Answers will vary but will include specific stories of how we can share grace and peace with the Church and with the entire world. Living in the Spirit looks like security that your real identity is as God's child. You have lavish grace and kindness to share with those who need it.

Day 14

1. Answers will vary but will include stories of trying to save grown children and other conflicts within the family. Control is an illusion from Satan that makes us feel as if we're helping when we are really taking over what is not actually ours to solve.

2. God takes so much better care of us and our families than we could ever take of ourselves. His purpose is always to bring us close to Him. On the other hand, we often want a specific outcome that serves us best in this moment.

Day 15

1. Answers will vary but will include different tools that women have used throughout their lives, including certain books and Bible study groups, church services and music that have been especially meaningful, retreats and other mountaintop experiences, specific friends or mentors, a routine of quiet time, a mission project, or a ministry.

2. Answers will vary but will include how solitude can change your time in prayer to God. Women might mention how much they appreciate the quiet. They might talk about how they find themselves noticing distractions more when they pray in busy surroundings. Mostly, they might talk about how prayer in solitude opens up freedom to spend much more time in prayer (without reminders about what else there is to do).

Day 16
1. Answers will vary and will probably include money, acceptance, love, work, medicine, and relationships. Reality always shows the truth about these idols.

2. Our true, divine Creator is all powerful, all knowing, all present, and all loving. Instead of communion and life with our true Savior, we settle for impotent gods. Our souls remain anemic as long as we put our hope in straw gods.

Day 17
1. Answers will vary but may include stories about how so many women put their faith in the roles, people, and things in their lives. Talk about how these earthly things will never be able to handle being worshiped because they were never intended to be.

2. When we worship earthly things and roles, we're trapping ourselves in more work, more neediness, and more desire. Our true Savior is the only one who delivers the deep love we are looking to experience. When we name God as our Father, we are living in our identity as His children. We're free from the systems that will trap us into more striving because we have a holy identity.

Day 18

1. Answers will vary but will include nudges from the Holy Spirit about connecting with people, tackling new adventures, and learning new skills.

2. Our heavenly Father equips us with everything good to do His will. He works in us that which is pleasing in His sight, through Jesus Christ. The description in Hebrews 13:20–21 includes Jesus as "the great shepherd" and "the blood of the eternal covenant" to remind us that God has already provided dramatically and perfectly for us.

Day 19

1. Answers will vary as women talk about situations in which they struggle to experience rather than analyze. Often, we wrongly put our trust in what we can understand intellectually rather than what we deeply know to be true. So often, we believe rules and right answers will save us from making any wrong moves. We long for the correct form and function to keep us safe. God's truth is grace, grace, grace. Even when we make mistakes, He forgives us over and over.

2. Answers will vary and will include different parts of the worship service.

Day 20

1. Answers will vary but may include stories of motherhood and life as a wife that feel very constricting and controlling. We all have stories about putting impossible demands on our time and energy only to buckle under the inhuman pressure. Encourage those stories, and then talk about how a life of grace is so much better and is how God designed us to live.

2. Answers will vary but will include that God's grace is enough for each of us and in every situation. Perfectionism is not the answer, and your tendencies toward perfectionism will pull you away from God's grace. Instead, keep turning to your true Savior for grace and to forgive yourself.

Day 21

1. Answers will vary but will include stories about how life makes us flexible, and we learn to keep learning and continue discovering.

2. Joseph relied on God and showed deep trust and dependence on God over and over. God shows us how the pivot points in our lives can teach us flexibility and to depend on Him.

Day 22

1. Answers will vary but will include women's different attitudes toward creating, building, inventing, and beautifying their lives. To stop consuming, consider what triggers you to do this. Practice working through the fear around creating.

2. Jesus taught that the way you spend your time, energy, and money determines what your treasure is. If you're collecting a lot of stuff, you're making this your treasure, and it's so temporary. Instead, center your life around what will last—your treasures in heaven.

Day 23

1. Answers will vary and will include discussion about helping loved ones, giving to others, and being humbled by the Spirit. We all need strengthening, and God provides for us this soul food through His Spirit.

2. These verses describe the human experience of living out spiritual transformation (Matthew 5:16; Philippians 4:8–9). Answers will vary with stories of how the Holy Spirit has changed the lives of participants.

Day 24

1. Answers will vary but may include stories about times when women have needed rest from their work. When your body needs rest, it feels worn out. You yawn, lie down, zone out, and do something that relaxes you. When your soul needs rest, you might feel empty, short-tempered, hopeless, anxious, and burnt out. Often our need to be productive is rooted in pride. We want to accomplish more to feel more valuable.

2. God is our Creator, and He knows what our bodies and our souls need. He tells us we need a day in which we can totally rest from our work. The Sabbath is part of our instruction manual for our bodies. Taking a break is exactly what we need and deeply desire; therefore, it's a gift.

Day 25

1. Answers will vary but will include stories and ideas of what each person would like to do during this season of her life. Encourage thoughts and exploration about what God has already done in participants' lives and how they have seen the Holy Spirit bless certain projects beyond all reason or expectation.

2. Answers will vary but will include that creative work can be a wonderful and joy-filled way to serve the Lord. Your inheritance is the free gift of salvation from your heavenly Father.

Day 26

1. Answers will vary but may include stories about seasons in which toxic relationships, struggles that poke at your deepest insecurity, and painful failures have convinced us to rely on the terrible solutions the world offers us.

2. Answers will vary but will include that time in prayer, Scripture, and worship will transform your mind to be like the Spirit. Bitterness, cynicism, and complacency settle in when we look to the world for wisdom and strength rather than God.

Day 27

1. Answers will vary but will include stories about what we have been taught about forgiveness. The truth about forgiveness is that it's a gift from God, and that means that it is not for us to control.

2. Forgiveness is spiritual and cannot be weighed, measured, analyzed, or calibrated. It's a gift because of the grace of God.

Day 28

1. Answers will vary as women discuss the ways the Holy Spirit has made this gift obvious in each of their lives.

2. All the gifts, no matter what they look like in our lives, are from the Holy Spirit and come to us in Baptism. He is the source; therefore, the gifts are for building up the people of God in His love and service.

Conclusion

1. Answers will vary but will include the role of mother, wife, employee, and daughter.

2. Answers will vary but will include that God calls you to share His Word with the world, and your security and hope are in the Holy Spirit going with you. You can share this all the way to the ends of the earth or through your actions and love for your neighbor.

Epilogue

1. Answers will vary, but women will share stories of when they feel anxious, sad, depleted, or otherwise like they cannot breathe. Also, encourage stories and comments about situations when women feel inspired and invigorated by the Spirit and able to breathe deeply. Talk about how our breath is a literal, constant reminder of God's strength in each of us.

2. Answers will vary as women share pictures of true, breath-filled life from their own stories. Talk about how Baptism is a life-giving event, how the Holy Spirit comes to us when the water is poured on our head and the Word of God is spoken over us, and how the Holy Spirit gives us faith to know that all these things are true for us. Encourage sharing about ways that women can live in the Spirit, and discuss God's promise of this new life. Pray together that as you finish this study, you will continue the habits of your best spirit-filled life.

ACKNOWLEDGMENTS

Mike: You are kindness. You serve and love like no one else. I love all the chapters with you, but this one most of all.

Catie: You are love. One million hugs, girl. All from you, and all exactly what I needed.

Sam: You are joy. I love your passion, your jokes, and your incredible perspective.

Elisabeth: You are faithfulness. Always reading, journaling, loving, and showing up. Always.

Nate: You are goodness. Your curiosity and enthusiasm are a model for me and for the world.

Mom and Dad: Fifty years of spiritual love for one another; a combined 150 years of living in the Holy Spirit; forty-six years as my spiritual guides. So blessed to have you both read this.

Aunt Katie: You have prayed for me through every season. I'm beyond grateful for every single one of your one million prayers. Breathe. John 20:22.

Mark and Marcilee: Your daily support means everything. Thank you for showing up.

Jen and Kenny Ward: Thanks for all the walks and conversation. Thanks for tolerating the sermons that became the pages of this book. Thanks for making me laugh.

Melissa and Scott Brignac: You are loyal, creative friends and a blessing straight from God. Thanks for all the conversation and prayers.

Connie and Sean Surcouf: You both love so well. Thanks for circling us in. We need your light and your example.

Amanda: It's not the same without you.

Ruth: Thank you for your time, editing eye, patience, and friendship.

For everyone who prayed for this book to be birthed: Thank you. I felt the power of your prayers, and I am forever grateful for them.

Elizabeth and Lindsey: You make my books come alive, and I love doing this with you. Thanks for being so good at all of it and working tirelessly to spread God's Word.

Peggy: Ah, friend. Thanks for decades together. What will this book become? Your fingerprints are all over it, and I can't wait to see.

Laura Lane and Holli Rolfes: Thanks for believing in this project.

Rob, Elizabeth, Anne: Your thoughts on creating and living a more Spirit-centered life keep inspiring me, and for that I am grateful.

Pastor Aaron: Your wisdom and generosity were such a help when I needed it. Thank you.

Sunday-Night Dinner Crew: Thanks for living out community and bringing the best food. Also, celery in everything!